BAREFOOT AT HEART

SANDY JONES shares her journey of self-discovery and tells us of the *Child Within* as she lives Its genuine liberation. Sandy was entrusted with William Samuel's literary legacy. William knew Sandy understood his metaphysical and spiritual teachings. She lives the childlike spirit his message is about wholeheartedly, unabashedly and fearlessly. Sandy is a starry-eyed, unbridled lover of Life and sails the cosmic fields of Light.

WILLIAM SAMUEL (1924-1996) was a renown spiritual master of metaphysics and higher Truth. He was known as the teacher's teacher. He passed along his knowledge with brilliance and humble humor as a writer and speaker for over 40 years. William Samuel devoted his life to the search for Truth. His quest to study at the fountainheads of the world's ideas took him twice around the globe, into its remotest places. His journey included time in China with Mr. Shieh the venerated Taoist Monk and, in 1944, a visit with Ramana Maharshi in India. Mr. Samuel's ability to instruct in a clear, simple and effective way has lead many to discover the fabled "peace beyond understanding."

In *Barefoot at Heart*, Sandy tells of her understanding in her own voice. She has found a unique way to bring her special gifts of the Child and Its enlightenment to others. She gives her heart to those who are interested in their own Self-discovery. Sandy is a writer, artist, surfer girl, untamed spirit and dancing-to-the-music shop owner of Jones & Company in Ojai, California.

Writing, Interviews and Artwork by Sandy Jones

Barefoot at Heart
The Alchemy of Love and the Power of Light

www.woodsongjournals.com

Works by William Samuel

The Child Within Us Lives!
A Synthesis of Science, Religion and Metaphysics

A Guide to Awareness and Tranquillity

The Awareness of Self-Discovery

Two Plus Two Equals Reality

The Melody of the Woodcutter and the King

www.williamsamuel.com

We invite the earnest reader's correspondence.

BAREFOOT AT HEART

The Alchemy of Love
and the Power of Light

SANDY JONES

Butterfly Publishing House
Ojai ♥ California

BAREFOOT AT HEART

Copyright 2015 by Sandy Jones

Butterfly Publishing House
307 North Montgomery Street
Ojai, California 93023, USA

FIRST EDITION, 2015

Library of Congress catalog

ISBN-13   978-1-877999-10-9
ISBN-10   1-877-999-10-5

Cover design by Alexa Bliss
Cover photography by Stefan Roth
Back cover text by Nicole Bliss Jones

Printed in the United States of America

*Dedicated to the fearless, victorious,
Beloved Child that brought me Home.*

Acknowledgments

"How beautiful upon the mountains are the feet of those who bring good tidings, who publish peace, who announce good news and who proclaim salvation and say to Zion, 'Your God reigns!' " –(Isaiah 52:7)

Finally, after many years of knowing I was supposed to write a book, I have done it. But, I want you to know, I could not have done it without every one of you standing here with your feet upon this Sweet Mountain with me.

My sincere and deepest gratitude to each and every one.

I thank my sweet daughter Alex who has been like an angel to me in every way. She is the girl with the answers and the know how. She is an amazing woman, working patiently with me to get this book perfected. And thanks to her dear husband Stefan for being there for both of us with his calm and grounded support.

Also my daughter Nicole for reading with an objective eye. Her intelligence and kindness work magic. She is a wonderful teacher, always allowing me to be who I am, accepting all my idiosyncrasy with love and wit. And my son Thomas for his strength, honesty and humor. I thank him for believing in me and trusting that I would arrive at something sagacious and wonderful, by doing it my way.

My friend Donovan Moore for his insight and brilliance. He was the spark that set me on fire to finally write this book. His generosity, knowledge and guidance have been magic.

I include Rich Hay who appreciated and encouraged me to share my wisdom. And Adrian for her kind support and her love for me, standing by me as a loyal friend. Dear Angie Chaney who created William's Youtube channel. She brings us such delight because she found the Child. She trusted me, she trusted her own inner guidance, and it is a joy to see her shine.

Also a thank you to Rick Archer for hosting my interview on Buddha at the Gas Pump. That was an enormous gift to me and to William Samuel's work. And to my friends Doug Manley, Lachlen French, John Weekly, Brian Hicks and John Bailey. They have all been helpful while teaching me so much.

Then, of course, there is William Samuel who blessed me with his foresight and inspiration, guiding me to re-discover the Child within. Without the Child none of this would have fallen into place as it did. Without the Child I'd not be who I am.

With deepest love for my precious husband, Jonesy, whose love continues to bestow upon me the ways and ability to do all I am given to do in the days to come.

And I thank the ungovernable Child of me. How I adore her. She sits next to God. And I can thank God for His Love for me and the Child I am.

Contents

❦

One | Prophecy and Old Letters

Two | Synergy

Three | Overtone

Four | Come to Think of It

Five | Unbound Love

Six | Stormy Seas

Seven | In the Stars

Eight | 4 A.M.

Nine | Black Leathers

Ten | Rockets

The way to tell it is to be it.
When we be it, we tell it with the most
wondrous effectiveness.

One

Prophecy and Old Letters

The aspen trees had turned golden and orange, shimmering and sparkling in the clear, high, mountain sunshine. The weather hadn't brought snow as of yet. The air was icy but the sun was keeping me warm. It was an early September day, 1996. I was sitting on my porch in Aspen rereading some old letters to me from William Samuel.

William was my spiritual guide and teacher for over twenty years. We corresponded often through letters. Much of what he wrote to me I see now was very prophetic. He did indeed have the gifts of a visionary. His words to me eventually did come to fruition. He was a true Master. I was blessed to know him.

The thing I really loved about William's teachings was that he always told me to look within my own heart. He would point me back to the childlike soul of myself. He said this tranquillity is acquired not through step-by-step methods, but rather by simplicity and honesty in a childlike approach.

Back then I was still searching. I knew he was right. I wanted to find this unfettered joy and peace he spoke of. I listened to him. I understood what this wise man was telling me, but I didn't have the whole picture yet. His letters to me implied that I was entwined in some kind of destiny. I could not see how my life and my purpose would all unfold. Now, these years later, now I know and now I understand entirely.

So, there I was on the porch reading his words of wisdom and encouragement and trying to glean all the insights I could. Trying to go over every word to see if there was some clue that I may have missed. Some deep meaning I'd not seen before. I had no idea then that the road I was on would require me to walk through such pain, sorrow and loss. Now I see that William knew exactly what would be required of me.

Over the years he often told me I had to keep trusting my Self, trusting my own heart. I did the best I could.

Reading William's letters again, he said, "Whatever you do, dear Sandy, trust the inner guide that leads you. It will lead you aright." He told me to praise all that has led me to It. In that, now I see, I had to one day give thanks for the things that broke my heart, the sorrow that tore me wide open and the anguish that took me down.

William said to me, "You will find the words for those ideas and visions that transcend humanhood and you will give your light to those who come to you." He said, "...and they *will* come." "You will be prepared for the eventuality." At the time I read that, I never considered that being prepared would entail facing the dark with nowhere to hide.

As I read those words over again, I was filled with wonder and doubt. I found the idea of a destiny enchanting and it felt true to my heart. But I didn't know what it would take to uncover and discover this raw, vulnerable, supernal essence of myself.

Well, now, these years later, now that I understand, it all makes sense in a whole new light. William knew I would have to walk, test, experience and live all those things he spoke of. I had to live all that has transpired.

He told me "within a few years, your knowledge of the Child within will be a saving grace to the world." William's words were staggering statements I couldn't even consider at the time. I knew he knew something I didn't know. I knew I could trust his words. But I had no idea what was up ahead. "You must learn your lessons well, Sandy, there will be quite a work in store for you." I couldn't imagine.

"The travel on the River of Life won't be easy – but you will make it. And more, you will chart the course and mark it on the map so that others can make the twists and turns beyond the shallows and sand bars and old shoals where the rocks are." It turns out I had to learn how to get myself out of the old shoals and shallows before I could show anyone else how to ride this River of Life. No, it was not easy, it was treacherous. But I did make it.

I didn't understand all he was telling me. So, I often read again his most generous letters he had sent to me over the years of our friendship. He wrote with such respect and love for me.

Now, finally, as I write this book all these years later, I know what he was saying and I know he was right. I have made my way to the peak, to the place from where I can soar free.

Now, I can map my own chart and give what I can of myself to you. I can share my journey, the way it was for me. I can give you my heart and my love. By simply expressing this Light of the Child's way, I can be the cheerleader championing you to the victory of finding the unbound freedom, peace and joy within yourself.

I write this book from the Child's heart I have found. I write this from the grace, eternal Light and true Love that saved me.

There is nothing more wonderful than to find this Love and Joy that comes to us from our Original Childlikeness because it *makes all things new*. There is a Light and Peace that is real and heals all things, it is the *Child That Lives*. It is the Delight and Joy of the Child that writes this book with me and shines her Love here.

Perhaps, through my words, I will strike a chord in your heart too, so you can remember the Eternal Light and Love that is the Living Truth of you. I can remind you of the Child that is your divine heritage. I will do my best to string the words just right and sing my own song in a way that might awaken the Child within you too.

Chart the Journey

I realize now, all these years later, our spiritual journey of Life has three phases, three steps to it. Three, not two. Not one. Three steps. Long steps mayhap, but three steps, if we do it right, if we are willing to yield to the Sweet Mystery.

Though there are ongoing changes at every moment, this Symphony of Life seems to have one grand melody in the overtone of a three-part song.

The three-part song goes something like this.

We are children first, carefree and innocent. The child of us is free spirited and fearless, unconcerned with the adult world of things. As children we live in a wonderland, directly enjoying life just the way it is.

Then we grow, and bit by bit we become adults. As adults, we lose our childlike wonder and become logical and reasoning. Our conceptual thinking takes over. Our purity of heart and our innocence gets covered up and put a way. Our fearless wonder and imagination is now buried deep within us. As adults we struggle with life, we are no longer free and unafraid. We think we are intelligent. We now see life as separate and apart from us. We see life as a possession of the body.

The third part of the song is the return to Peace, the Holy Ground, the Shikinha. This comes when we rediscover, return

4

and claim our own pristine childlikeness once again. More, we actually become that child again, but this time knowing who we are. This time recognizing the gift as the innocence and purity of the real and holy Child we are. This time fully aware of what we almost lost and rejoicing in the pure joy of having the Child's unbound awareness returned to us, as us, living in peace and happy laughter once again.

Little Melody

As children in linear time we were bright and charming and unafraid. We were funny and cute, bold and brave, guiltless and unashamed. We had a mind of our own and wanted to do things our way. We didn't want mommy or daddy to tell us what to do and we liked it when we felt self-reliant. We were curious and inventive, creative and carefree. We were also innately kind and giving, tender and caring.

That's how it was for me. I was a happy little girl. I loved life and the engaging everyday things. I loved my big grey cat. I loved my teddy bear, my cowboy boots, my twirly skirt. I loved to dance and laugh. I loved the stories and songs I would play on my little record player.

I remember, I was only a baby, no more than 3 years old, and I would sit on the floor upon that green woven-cotton rug and listen intently to the story of *Celeste the Little Melody*. It was an old used record my mother bought for me at the Goodwill. She loved rummaging the second-hand stores for rare treasures. And she often found them. I would play that beat-up 78 over and over again. I'd listen to that musical story, enchanted by the tale of adventure and love, Celeste and the Singing City and the Charming Prince Cello. I would gaze, delighted, at the pictures on the record cover. My imagination was so vivid and alive. There was the Police Whistle, the Little Brown Mouse, the Knights and the Big Fat Cook. And Celeste, sweet Celeste, the beautiful lonesome little tune. She just didn't belong to any-body. One day Celeste heard of a far-off city where everybody had a melody all his own. "That's the place for me." So off she went to the Singing City.

As a little child just sitting there on the living room rug, my mind and my heart were captivated as I listened to the sounds, the music, all the instruments of the orchestra. My imagination felt the characters come alive.

Well, yes, we are all delightful, innocent children first. It goes like this for every one of us. Children are beautiful little souls in heart and spirit.

The Cover-Up

Then, little by little we find out things are not as we think they are. We begin to grow up, compare, learn to make judg-ments, and get afraid of making mistakes or looking foolish. We hide the child, we put her away, we bury her somewhere deep inside of us.

For me, I do believe the covering up of my divine innocence and light began when I started going to school. I was eager and enthusiastic at first. I wanted to answer the questions the teacher asked, and found myself so dismayed when I was told my answer was wrong. I felt fear. I felt wrong for the first time. I felt ashamed. I stopped raising my hand to answer. I began to hide my unique individuality. I looked around and I wanted to be like the other kids.

Yes, somewhere it begins, we start comparing ourselves. Realizing I was not doing quite as well in my studies as the other kids. Feeling as if the teacher liked the other children more, as if they had something I needed to have – and – well, little did I know, they were learning to think the same things I was. They too were burying their own childlike wonder and divine beauty and individuality.

Some of them may have learned to play the role of adult a little faster, but they too were losing the sweet Light of the holy Child as they tried to fit in – so on it goes. It is the way it goes. We just start growing up and little by little the pristine, innocent beauty of the child gets covered, muzzled, hidden, wrapped-up and buried deep within us. Our childlike wonder and our divine light goes dim, smothered under the cloak of adulthood. We forget what it even felt like to be a child.

All of that is just as it is supposed to be. As Henry David Thoreau said, "Not until we are lost do we begin to understand ourselves."

Eventually, slowly, imperceptibly, not even really noticing it, I was no longer the carefree, bold little girl I once was.

And so my spiritual soul-searching began.

I was tender, and wanted to be strong. I didn't realize how very beautiful that tenderness was. I wanted to be free to be myself, the person I used to be, but I had lost myself it seemed. Of course, that is what happens when the adult-conceptual mind takes over. We lose our connection to our own inner free spirit, our light, the wholeness and beauty of ourself and our truth.

Eventually I adjusted and the ways of the adult became just fine by me. I learned to fit in and fit in very nicely. But my search for Truth continued. The search for God, asking the perennial questions, had begun.

Return to the Child

"I learned that every mortal will taste death, but only some will taste life." –Rumi

My good intentions along with my destiny led me to a man, a spiritual teacher, a master metaphysician, a teacher's teacher, who would show me the way back to exactly what I was looking for – my Self, the Child, Reality, Identity and Peace. This master teacher's name was William Samuel. He became my guide, my mentor and my very dear friend.

He told me our only hope to know an unknowable God comes from a thorough knowledge of the Self, which is made in God's image and likeness. How else can Ineffability be understood, if not by the thorough knowledge of the Entity made in Its image. We are always coming back to the Self.

Thus, because of him, because of my sincerity and honesty, because of the love that was deep within me, because of that little light of optimism that never went out – I did find the direction, I did find my way back.

The answers came when I returned to my Self. I returned to the pristine peace and tranquility of my Childlike heart and soul. I reclaimed the little girl I was and she was very willing to take my hand and lead me once again.

I discovered this holy Child of my Self sits as close to God as anyone will ever get. She sits at the hem of Reality. The wonder and beauty of this childlikeness I found again is so much better, richer, sweeter, easier, and more peaceful, joyous, whole and familiar than what I thought "enlightenment" and finding God or Truth would be. And this is real. It is real.

The Child of me was still here, pure and unharmed, still unblemished, innocent, and free. Nothing had ever happened to that prefect part of my Self.

She is with me now, again, all these years later. She comes with many gifts for me. More, she becomes my freedom and my joy, she is my own personal savior. She knows what Reality *is* and *what it is not.* She knows *what is shadow* and *what is Tree* and she lives them both at once, as one, in perfect harmony and love for It all. There is no discarding anything included here in Life. There is only to understand and love. Life, wonderful Life, is real and not real, both and greater than either.

Like my teacher William Samuel told me, the return to the Child is the return to the Holy Spirit, the Messiah, the Light of understanding this world, the return to Love.

This Child knows all about this world and how to navigate its labyrinths. She takes me back to the eternal love, the fearless love I started with. She brings me peace, understanding and un-bridled happiness. And yes, she has taken me back home again. Home is now the very heart of the Universe entire.

It is my joy to share my Child Heart with you. It is my unre-stricted love that wants to chart my journey for you. To remind you of the Child *you are* and aways will be. I'd like my story to lead you to your own discovery, allow you to find your original nature, the Child that transcends divisions, paradox and limited perceptions. As the Child, we find understanding and the joy of life returns to us once again.

Some Day, One Day, Maybe

Because this sweet unbound Child has come back to me, I find life to be, once again, so very beautiful and rich and divine. I find that my world feels just like it did when I was a little girl. It is extraordinary and wonderful.

This energy of Love, this heart that is the Child's calls me to live with the deepest integrity and it holds me to some of the highest responsibility.

I write this book to the holy Child of my Self which is the Child of you too. I write to the children of the world who can come alive and live again. I write to all those whom I have been given in this lifetime, to those I love, and as William Samuel said, to the weary travelers down the way who might find me. I write to those who seek true freedom and genuine liberation through the honest light and living truth of Self-discovery.

I will tell you what William Samuel told me; he said to trust your own heart "because for you there will never be words more important anywhere than the words that come from yourself — written or spoken." He is exactly right.

Alchemy

When I first began the book, I had to just leap in and start writing. I couldn't do it with a plan in mind. I couldn't find the plan. Yet I knew I was called to write.

Fortunately, by the time I got to the end of all those words that were unleashed, the end turned out to be the beginning. That always seems to be the way I get somewhere; I start from where I want to go even though I'm not there. I really don't know how else to do things. I am open, trusting, impulsive and spontaneous, which can be dangerous.

From doing what I don't know how to do, I end up knowing how to do it. I guess that's called learning. I love to learn.

When I was about 3 years old I learned to swim by leaping in the pool totally unafraid. I loved the water. Tossing myself into things with sheer abandon is what I do when I am in love. In love with that swimming pool I would toddle over to the water and just leap in.

My dad would then have to drop everything and jump in the pool and lift me to the side. I actually do remember that. I also seem to recall that it didn't take more than a few leaps and I was dog paddling on my own.

I still live like that. I am in love. Where else can I be? So, I just throw myself in and trust that I can do whatever it is I decide to do. Sometimes there's that first moment of "Oh no, what have I done!" but somehow I rise to the surface, take a breath and learn. Life lifts me up, holds me and shows me the way.

Now my book is almost finished. The whole unfolding of it turned out to be rather magical. I am surprised with what has evolved from the rambling explosion of words. Lovely words, really a profuse bounty pouring from my untamed heart and my illimitable soul, but I had no idea where they were going. I just let them flow. Now, down the road a ways, I have something quite tangible and whole.

I can trust my heart, and this always abiding, innate sense of faith in Life being the common denominator which can never be harmed or changed or lost. It's all synergy and magic.

No Chronology

There is no chronological timeline or way this Self-discovery happened for me. There is no logical order to this unfolding story I present here. Past, present and future co-exist and collide at every moment.

Self-discovery, happiness, freedom, it happened on many levels, gradually sometimes, quickly, sometimes in a flash, in the twinkling of an eye, sometimes slowly, sometimes – but mostly layered, deeply layered. The dawning of Light happened just as my teacher said it would, "line upon line, precept upon precept, here a little, there a little." Yet, because I was always this Child, it happened all at once. Suddenly it was clear. I was transformed. I was free. I was always here, I never went away.

So, the story is multifaceted at once. It cannot be told in any logical or linear way really. I will give you the Heart of the story. The power of the story. The sweet juice of the story. Don't try to organize this story by time or logic.

Like a flower that blooms, this flower is already contained in the seed, from the beginning. The flower existed in full bloom right inside the seed, from the beginning. As I was blooming, I didn't know any of this was happening in the way it did.

That's how this Self-discovery came to me. It came slowly. It came at many levels. It came horizontally sometimes, vertically at other times. It came from within and it came from out there somewhere, offered to me from others, brought to me through love, through synchronicity, through Life. Often, without even knowing a transformation was happening, it was happening.

And one day, I was free, completely free. I was the spirit of that little girl skipping along the edge of the water, barefoot on wet sand at the beach, I was free. Truly, I am that little girl once again. Vitality, beauty, unleashed love, laughter and enthusiasm move me now.

Contradictions and paradoxes no longer exist, yet they are all included and I include them in my words. Because the Infinite is not limited to logic and reason, it is Illimitable, beyond logic and reason, it is an ongoing mystery. Logic and reason are not thrown out, but they often yield to the heart. Living from the Heart is living from the unabashed, random, intuitive, illogical, wild joy of this Mystery. The Infinite can't be limited. It would not be Infinite if it was bound only to making sense or fitting into anything orderly or disciplined.

Yes, the Truth is all those things, but it has to be more, and greater than more, because God, Divine Mind, is Illimitable and cannot be confined to any point of view.

So the Living Truth is also random and scattered in aimless wonder and without purpose. It is not logical. All means All. I find this unbridled realization to be the freedom of my laughter and delight. I love Life in all its Infinite, uncensored, haphazard, childlike, untamed beauty. I am seeing life from on high, as I see the wide range of so much, as it is all-inclusive below me. I stand here between heaven and earth. Here it is both. Always both and yet one. And the paradox vanishes into thin air.

Here, included in my view, I can see that all the paths, the many paths, every path, any path leads up to the same exact point on the Mountain, here where I am. Here, where the true Self stands unbound and free.

Magnetic Wonders

Magnetism, it's all magnetic. The world is magnetic. Life, I notice now, seduces me, allures me, wants me. Life's beauty is irresistible. Life is to be experienced, felt and enjoyed. Now, I listen to my heart, my soul, my five senses that keep me in touch with my world. I am all these sensations and I am more than this body. I have more than five senses too. I am a combination of sensuosity and an alchemy of Love. I am intuitive, I have six senses and I have even more as each sense combines to make greater magic.

It is a kind of feeling I feel. *Something tells me.* And I have learned to trust it.

Throughout my life I have been pulled toward exceptional people and they toward me. People are magnetic. Magnets hold information. This unseen, unspoken information is exchanged between us. I am captivated. The attraction is mutual.

My Life unfolded the way it did because of these marvelous attractions to uncommon and exceptional people. I am quite sure these magical and transformational relationships were written before time, written in Heaven – meant to be. I love them all. They are a part of me and in my heart always.

I can see this world is intelligent, all-knowing and mystical. This world is a world of love, beauty and ongoing, flowing Light of Information. This Ineffable Divine Intelligence, being this Life and Light, knows what we need and It knows how to bring these things to us.

I sense that the good and loving people in my life have been with me for many lifetimes. They return to me, and I to them. Love connects us. Love is the magnetic pull. We are here for each other to give and guide and help each other if we need. I can see those I have loved always return to me. We find each other throughout the many lifetimes. There is an eternal bond of love that seems to magnetize, pull us together through each new lifetime.

You are here in my life as the tangible depiction of love, as I am for you. This world of body, form, matter is perfect and to be cherished. We really are here to love one another and our world as ourself. It's easy when we understand it.

In order to leap in and do what I am here to do, peace and honesty are essential. This living equanimity and integrity has found me. I have no fear. I feel the bright sunshine in a clear wakefulness of Something Wonderful unfolding and I am feeling urged to complete this interface now, to fulfill my destiny.

Untamed Wildflowers

And, this might be helpful to know, I'm really not an any-thing, not left or right. I have no political affiliation. I belong to no organized religion or ideology, Eastern or Western. Well, I kind of have my own unorganized theology that sits in my heart like a welcoming garden of rambling, untamed wildflowers. I am fond of not being fenced in. I don't follow Buddhism or any other "ism." I am, at this point in my life, just one big open heart. I am living a sort of undefined love and I love this world of mine. I am not afraid to be who I am. I am here to bring you my heart, however that might transpire. I realize, since doing this for some time now, that this world loves me back and brings me all I need for whatever sweet purpose I might serve.

Words Lift the Gloom

William's letters were always valuable at nudging me toward myself. It took me many years to find my own way of sharing what I understood, but I found it. Words are powerful. Words can illustrate ideas so that others might climb this starry ladder to the higher Light of Self and find a grand new Joy. There are words that can reveal the joy and light often hidden behind the intellect. As William said, "Reading for information is an effort but reading for confirmation is a joy." I write because I love you.

"January 7, 1982
"How to answer such a lovely letter, dear Sandy? Right from your journal notebook.
"Truth, restricted to writing and words, is such a small part of Truth it is no wonder you feel that few others would under-

15

stand. It is difficult to get those words to do justice to such a subject – and there are those who, like some Eastern and MidEastern Lights, who wouldn't even think of trying. They might talk a bit about it, but write? Never.

"But words CAN crack the shell. Words CAN lift the gloom of depression. Words CAN touch us at points that send us on our way happily more cognizant, more alert, more grateful.

"I've had a feeling from the first that you would write one day – and publish! Please set your cap to do so. You have so much to say that hasn't been said well enough yet.

"YES, 'it works for all problems and difficulties – worldwide and personal. It could 'Save the World' – but it seems futile, in some ways, to even think in such Grand, Humanitarian ways....'

"It may SEEM that way, gentle Sandy, but don't you forget that the 'world' who accepts and rejects and seems to have many minds of its own are all part of the illusion of separate minds and egos. Really, there is but one point of acceptance or rejection – your own solipsistic Selfhood, within which all other 'minds' are but your own myriad points of view – all necessary to make plain 'the many.' While we may never see a world where the appearances of egos agree, we can certainly see one where a new Idea is introduced, examined, put to the test – and a grand new Joy overspread everything. And why not? Why not?

"The words that I don't find, perhaps you will. The idea I can't illustrate and make clear, you can. So set your cap to 'Write it on the tables so that those who readeth it may run!'

"I can warn you that this 'work' is not easy. There is heat and light where the Fire is struck – but the fuel of that fire is 'old think'– cherished opinions, institutional foundations, monetary systems, and all that the world holds dear. But it doesn't have to be cataclysmic beyond our own personal sense of things. We may jolt the entire dream but it is only one sleeper who stops dreaming. Us.

"Thank you for your Christmas letter and for the Christmas Light it contained. Please write as often as you wish. Tell others of our books. Take care — and keep writing in your journal. Hold tight to the idea of publishing!!

"Tender, honest love

"To you and yours....... Bill Samuel"

Kaleidoscope

Life is filled with change and beauty like a kaleidoscope. I am the spirit of childlike joy that understands and delights in the many changing colors life keeps twisting and turning into this unending beauty. The wonder and mystery of this kaleidoscope of life is infinite. I will enjoy the experience of these changes. Nothing is ever the same, yet life is always showing us back to the love that moves all things.

Infinite, the kaleidoscope is filled with radiant shards of gems and jewels, colored in every combination we can imagine and beyond, always changing. Life is beautiful. Things change, like the images in the kaleidoscope. With every twist the light pours through and the view is never the same. The exploding vision is always dazzling, awesome and marvelous. It is divinely perfect in its multiplicity. Nothing but beauty abounds here.

I have discovered I am not the changing jewels in the kaleidoscope. I am not one of the many multi-fractals of colors and images moving and exploding in endless visions.

Now I see I am the Light that shines upon those moving shards. I am the Light of the changeless love that is not altered by the movements of the swirling colors appearing to dance and sparkle, spin and fall into such wondrous designs before me. Life and I are one Identity. Life loves me. I am Its Lover. We two create the experience of Life Itself. We two come together to bring form into being. The Self I am is the sensuous, delectable beauty of Life. I bring Life into tangible experience. This Self I am is the very experiencing of life with all these senses turned on. My soul is passionate for life, for all of it, the feelings, the thoughts, the imagination, the ideas and the earthly delights.

Yes, the earthly delights, to breathe in deeply the smell of fresh cut green grass on a summer day. To touch silk and velvet. To feel the cool breeze on my skin. To savor a bite of dark chocolate and whipped cream. Yes, and hold a long stemmed crystal glass of wine, and taste something holy. This body and my beloved in my arms, what pleasure this is. I will rejoice for this Self that can know such passion and feelings. To love life. It is the joy of living, the joy of food and music, of laughter and song. It is Love. That seems fine by me. My God is enjoying being this alive, this enchanted by me, my God is dancing with me. I smile, happy to have broken free. Fearless now. Loving this life as the very Identity of all that I am.

I have this deep intuition that is felt in the passion that moves my soul.

I am the Heart of this one changeless Love. It is Life and it is the living presence of all that I am. Presence, sweet Love, it never leaves me. I am consistent, immutable, as Life is the very identity I am, my Self. I am the very Life of these moving colors that spin within my Light.

I am Love, and Love has dominion. Love reigns supreme. I am comfort and wholeness as Life is this beauty of my flesh, my soul, my heart. Love is untouched by the coming and going of the ever-changing show before my eyes. Love, so close, so deep in my being, intimate, powerful and real.

Yet, sweet Life, I know that without the dancing colors and fractal echoing fragments reflected as these images of changing beauty, there would be no kaleidoscope at all, no Life at all, no love at all, no world.

Life, I love you. I am living in the wonder of being entwined in your lovely being of spinning delight and joyful magic.

Always yours –

Desert Night

The vibrations of heaven play in my mind. I hear harmonic tunes turning me into living poetry as I am painting love songs on the canvas of the sky. Your words merge like music as my ideas sing to you in melodic sounds and soft, silky, quiet tones of love. I can feel Life touch me. I am willing, as the wind unbuttons my heart and blows me into bliss.

You came slipping, easing slowly into my heart, awakening these forgotten delights, like smooth pink ice cream melting into dreams, dreams written thousands of years ago, unwrapped here, now, as gifts from eternity.

I remember how I held tight to you, riding on your speeding motorcycle. We rode wandering through the red desert, through the thundering storm and found our way to a little cafe along the road.

Wet and happy we went inside. The warmth of love between that gust of cold air and the sparkling fire heating the room, was combusting in our senses to ignite us into flames. Love, love alone is the powerful elixir. We are taken by this alchemy and magic.

The large stone fireplace flickering in flames of golden light casting boldly dancing shadows on the walls. We drink warm brandy. We sigh, we laugh. Your smile shines within my eyes.

My joyful benevolence soothes you. You see your own beauty dazzles my soul.

In a few hours the storm passes. We hear the silence. We go outside. Looking up into the clear, infinite wonder of desert's depth of dark that holds us, we are fearless. We smile. Looking up to see the stars twinkle in diamond-blue sparks shimmering brightness, we hold hands, we head out into the infinity that shines light from heaven to earth and back.

As long as the stars are above you –

Time

Time? What is time?

And, what time is it?

Time is a glorious mystery. No one knows *what* time is.

And no one knows *what time it is.*

Some say it's always now, and that's true. Some say time heals, and that's true too. The fact that times heals is such a sweet truth.

But yet, some see the effects of time and don't like time at all, as the body grows old and they grow weary.

Some say it is time for the harvest, that the divine quantum clock has struck midnight and we are at the dawn of a new day. It feels like that to me. William Samuel certainly thought so:

"The world has begun the travail that ends in the birth of the Child within – Messiah, Redeemer, Savior! – closer than breathing, closer than fingers and toes, not far off but here all the while. What is more, we will see THEN that this Event, the 'Birthing,' has every bit, each step of the way, been foreseen by the lights and prophets, Eastern and Western, above and below,

first and last, male and female. More, all of this will be WON-
DERFUL – precisely what has been called for from the begin-
ning – naught but GOOD going on – the REBIRTH of the
Original Image of Godhead."

I see this thing called time as the evidence of the timeless,
changeless living presence of God. Time is the evidence of God
made visible, seen, witnessed, experienced, lived, touched, felt
and known. Time cannot affect that which is transcendent, God
or this Child.

Heaven on Earth

I have been very fortunate. I grew up in a small beach town in
Southern California. The town aptly named Corona del Mar. I
wander back in memory of how life was sweet and easy those
many years ago. For me, that beautiful place really was *The
Crown of the Sea*. It seemed to me every day sparkled like royal
jewels. There was light and beauty in everything.

My days of childhood there were perfection. I spent all
summer at the beach. Even when I was very young, before I went
to school, my mother would take us to the beach to play. She
would pack up beach towels and umbrella, lunch and beach toys.
We'd climb in her car and she'd drive down the steep hill to Big
Corona.

At the beach, we would play for hours near the waves, toes in
the water, gathering seaweed and digging in the wet sand.

As I got a little older, in the summer, as very young girls, my
friend Julie and I would spend our days at China Cove. It was
named China Cove because on the beach there was a lovely rose-

colored Chinese house with a wonderful green, oriental-style roof. The China House is gone now. Demolished.

Julie's mother would pack us a picnic lunch and she always included those big pink marshmallowy cookies for us.

There were no waves at this beach. It was like a secret spot because it was facing the inside of the bay. Secluded and quite private, it was a perfect beach for tiny children.

We'd play in the water for hours, floating on our rafts, laughing and giggling, making up games, singing and talking. The day was so full of joy, doing nothing, accomplishing nothing, getting nowhere, drifting, splashing in sunshine and salty water.

Well, much to my surprise these years later that little girl of those days has returned to me. She is here in my heart once again. I am astounded by this and grateful. Yes, I am that child anew. And I am free, drifting, playing, laughing, making up games and singing my heart's unbridled joy. The Child, the one who sits so close to Life, she has returned to me.

She brings me the sweetest delights, she brings me this magic that lives in the simplicity of real untamed Love. I am free and fearless and alive to this whole sea of wonder and beauty that holds me now. She takes my hand and she watches over me, she knows exactly how to navigate this world for me. I listen to her and she shows me the way. She is connected to Something Wonderful. She brings me unexpected surprises too – surprises even sweeter than those big pink marshmallow cookies.

Days of the Child

As I grew older, during the school year I ignored my school work entirely. I wasn't interested in sitting inside a classroom.

My independent nature didn't want to be told what to do or when to do it. I couldn't wait for the final bell to ring so I could run free and be out on my own.

After school or on weekends, I enjoyed exploring the dusty, dirt roads and the hills behind our home. I loved being alone. I loved rock hunting, spying the sparkling stones along the way. I liked getting near the strange gullies and peering down, deep into their ancient forms. I was ever fascinated by these earthy, strange crevasses that had been carved by rushing rains over many years. They were a mystery. I liked mysteries. I still do.

Out exploring the hills, free and wandering alone, being in nature was what I loved most. Everything was real and alive.

My childhood home was backed up against the Irvine Ranch hills, open space sometimes used for grazing cattle, more often just the wild, ever-changing beauty of the fields. Life was out there. I could hear the soft cooing sounds of the quail in the mornings. If they had brought the cattle in, then I could hear the peaceful lowing of the cows at night.

I loved to romp free through the beauty of the wild grass. And sometimes they would plant crops out there. So, in the fall the thrashers would come and gather the huge fields of barley occasionally grown there.

Then there were the old oaks at the top of the hill. Always so lovely. Two lone beauties standing together like sentinels. I'd hike up to be near them. Hawks would soar and the mocking birds sang their lovely melodic tunes. Life out in this natural beauty mingled with my uninhibited soul and made me happy. I liked to wander far away, meandering, investigating the sage and cactus, sometimes with friends, sometimes by myself. Fearless and daring, I loved it all.

Walking without aim, enjoying the days, would always lead to something of interest. Just the feeling of it all, the fragrance of the earth, the sea air, and the wonderful pungent scent of sage that permeated my clothes, my hands, as I pushed through the wild brush.

From the top of hills I could see the ocean. It would be my beautiful, big, dark wintery grey sea on stormy days, covered with whitecaps dancing in the winds.

It was my glistening, sparkling sea of changing colors and shifting scenes, sometimes decked with sail boats, sometimes serene and calm, sometimes blustery and windblown, but always there in all its enchanting, capricious beauty.

In the summer the sea was lit up by the sun's light reflecting upon the moving waters. The vast waters of my sea on a hot summer day would be aglitter in lights, blinking, twinkling on and off, shining a radiance so magical and brilliant.

All the seasons, my sea was there. Changing, moving and always there. I would stand high upon those hills and watch it as I was completely beguiled by the ocean's immense and glorious presence, power and beauty.

Being outside, out of class rooms and far from restrictions suited my soul. My life was full and rich and beautiful. Yes, I was very fortunate and Life is good.

Mirrors and Reflections

My mother had a four-way mirror in her dressing room. As a little girl I was fascinated by this set of mirrored doors. They opened in a way where I could stand in a certain place and see my reflection duplicated to infinity. Left was right and right was left. It appears to be a chorus line of little girls all in a row and moving at the same exact time.

I would do a dance in the mirror and all the little copies of me would do the same dance at exactly the same time. And I wondered if those little girls were perhaps following me by just a nanosecond. I tried to fool them and moved real fast so I could catch them following behind me. I did believe they were following me. I was quite sure I had caught a glimpse of them moving one slight moment after I did.

I was enjoying the infinite, fractal duplicates of myself, all the way to forever as I peered down the line of images, images, images of images each reflecting the reflection. Each reflecting another image. It all intrigued me.

There was something I knew that they did not know. Something I was that they were not. There was something I was the authority of and they were not. I had dominion. I was the mover of them all. They could not do anything without me. But how could I be sure they were not there in the mirror until I showed up. Did they ever dance while I was away? Were they hiding in the closet in my mother's dressing room and only stepped out when I came to see them?

That row of blonde, curly-haired little girls all doing exactly what I did was so captivating to me.

That chorus line to infinity was quite the entertainment on a foggy Saturday morning. I'd dance and they'd all dance. I'd wave and they'd all wave back at me.

I loved my mother's dressing room. There were silk party dresses hanging in the closet, luscious fabrics, textures, colors and design, all infatuating me. I imagined her out at some royal gathering. High heeled shoes with ribbons and straps, such things of beauty I adored. Her perfume bottles, so exotic and alluring sitting upon the marble basin top. There was the soft oriental carpet, a tapestry of magentas, greens and gold for my little bare feet to dance on. I liked spending my time there, alone with my reflections in that quiet space. I had a vivid imagination, I envisioned so much mystery, all in 3-D technicolor.

Now it all comes clear. Life is like that four-way mirror. God is the Source, the Original Unseen Dancer. This world of matter is the Living Evidence of the Divine Mind, the Infinity of God's Images and Likeness.

Which brings up the Large Hadron Collider measuring time, trying to find the First Cause. The physicists are searching the images in order to find the original *Source* of existence.

Physicists are getting closer to finding the First Image. The First Image is like the real little girl who stands in front of the mirror. The scientists are searching for the source of all things, the cause of the universe. They will find the Light of Reality is their very Self, the Life of You and Me, reflecting all we see. In other words, the physicists are about to realize the Self *they are* is the one they are colliding with at the beginning of time.

They will find they are the Child or offspring of the Primary Mover. They will find the first image, the one closest to God. They will find they are the one they were seeking.

Nothing moves in the world of reflections without the First Image, the Child. The Self, Who I Am. This Child is the one touching the Original Love, the Illimitable One that stands in front of the Mirror. The Child, our very Life, is the first image.

Life is God's Love made evident. The journey through the images eventually arrives at the One that precedes all this. We find the Sweet Simplicity of our Self, this Alone, Single One.

Love and Its simplicity prevails as this joy and my delight. What a beautiful experience Life is – I get to Live.

Life/God's Light and I are dancing. It is a wonderland. Life is magical. I am a little girl again, living in this enchanted world, playing in the mirrors of my Divine Mother's dressing room. God laughs. God loves to see me dancing. We are connected in the Divine of My Being. There is no separation between Life and God and me and my world and those I love.

As the Child, the Soul, I find my Self standing here next to God. The Child is the one closest to the Source.

And yes, sweet to know that I am not God. Only God is God. There is only one First Cause. All else is that original Life or Mind being reflected, images, ongoing, all the way to infinity.

Yet without the first image, you and me, the soul of us, the Awareness we are, the Child we are – there would be no world at all. "I and my Father are one, but my Father is greater than I."

So, now, I see. Now I am fearless and I dance and watch the rest of myself dance too. I am the dancer. I am the song. I am God's living music. I am His Light and Life enjoying Life. I am Love. I am His only begotten Son, Child of God, Holy Child. I am a little girl with a tender heart and soft giggles of innocence and joy. I am a Child, free and fearless, guileless, unashamed to live from the radiant light of God's perfect reflections, all the way, enamored, delighted, as far as I can go – all the way. God and I are one. God is the Illimitable Light that is behind everything I see. Here in my Heart, God and I smile at each other. I am the world I walk through.

In love always –

Divine Equation

A fount of love has been tapped. I pour myself out to you because my love is infinite and always here. I cannot hold it back. The ingenuity of love becomes evident. Love finds ways through what seems like walls, or dead ends. Love finds ways through what feels like treacherous territory. Love knows how to move through the impossible. God is Love and God is Reality. Reality is Love. Love is the magic elixir. Love changes everything. Love is about giving. Love gives and knows what to give. Love leaves the confines of ideologies, doctrines, dogma and the limitations of rules. Love is freedom. Love makes it easy to see in new ways. Love and freedom go hand-in-hand. The Truth resides right here as the very Identity I am. Each of us can put ourself here as this Self-same Identity I am.

This beautiful River I found swept me up and takes me along with roaring force. I am riding on the waters of pure joy. I don't know where this River goes. My spirit is free, alive, creative and watchful as I am moved through the rapids, caught in the eddies, pushed onward over the falls, moving down this river of life. I am open to see what happens next, what happens now.

The Big Boys

Hanging out with my older brother and his friends was an adventurous way to spend the weekends during the school year. The boys were always looking for something new and exciting to do. I felt privileged they would let me join them. They never seemed to mind that I was there. I felt very accepted and that they enjoyed having me around. I sometimes preferred to be with them rather than the girls my age.

Being with the big boys was thrilling. Something about their boldness, their freedom and their energy I loved. Now I see they made me conscious of my rough and tumble self, the fearless rebel of me, the wild gambler in me. They found things to do that were on the edge of danger. I liked that. They talked about things that kept me excited, interested and curious. I listened and I learned. We would take turns on the Flexi-Flyer speeding down the street, flat out, no control on the steep grade. We never calculated our chances of meeting up with an on coming car. We assumed luck was always in our favor and it always was.

The big boys and their bb guns. I loved the guns and the bows and arrows too. I loved shooting tin cans and aiming for the bull's eye on the haystack. I had good aim, I was a good shot.

The boys could always find something wild, inventive and a bit dangerous to do at any moment. Their daring was captivating and I learned a lot hanging out with the boys. They had no fear and would often be close by the edge of trouble. I just followed without fear. None of us thought about it. It was the irresistible curiosity and excitement of being young and unafraid of life. I had the kind of curiosity that wanted to try things for myself. Life calling us to risk, to gamble, to dare. I liked the call. It was the innate Spirit of the Child, the one true Light, that knows in fact no matter what we do everything is really alright.

Natural Heart

There is a natural heart. There is this Child within us that knows the Truth. It lives and responds deeply and intuitively to Life. It is the soul of us. It is the pristine mind, pure and shining clear. It is a way of Living. It is who we are at the very core of our Self. It is both within us and transcendent. It is understanding what is and what is not, both at once.

Everyone knows what this is. It is the authentic Self within us. The one who dares to stand alone and free. The one that is not beholden to false images of ridged ideas of perfection. This is the confident Self that lives from the genuine, honest integrity of individual expression. The authority is within you.

There is no point in keeping this Light from shining in our world. Finding the Child is to uncover the one we are meant to express. We are born with this divine imprint. We can let it up and out, thus benefiting all concerned.

29

This individual shines with the qualities and attributes of those everlasting and eternal verities – those traits of character that make for real beauty and light that is the true unspoiled heart of us. We are, each one of us, the Sons of God.

And yes, this Child I am lives with abandon, not giving two hoots in hell what the political or religious ambassadors might think.

Heart and soul come together with the crystalline mind to form a triad of wholeness and power, like a holy trinity.

Here, I am dancing in the barroom of the universe. The cosmic rock band plays. We hear those marvelous melodies that turn us on, get us moving, light our fire. We harmonize. We move to the rhythm of the music bestowed to us by the Eternal Song Writer.

We become the artist, the poet, the music of this passionate body, full of enthusiasm and the warmth of understanding.

Now we are full of life again, like a child, full of spontaneity, happiness, sincerity, humor and honesty.

The real of us is adaptable and courageous. The nature of our true Self shines, playful with a love that is pure, it "thinketh no evil."

We know we have the right to be ourself, unique, nonconforming expressions of the truth of this holy, cosmic universe that shines in this light of our minds, our eyes, our imaginings, our wonder and our love.

When I let my heart open fully to Life, to the divine light that flows like a holy river, I am set free to move through this *earth life* clear-eyed, in full stride and unafraid. I am touched by a joy and freedom that lets me take life as I find it. I'm not trying to make life fit into a mold, a format, a slot. Not now, not any more. Now my soul is free and is living the pure joy, making it worthwhile for others as I make it worthwhile for myself.

With this natural Self, I am living from the circumference of my being. I am living way out here beyond the fences. And yet, I am in the center, strong and steady as I found this Golden Point in the middle.

It is our nature to be an artist all the time, being an artist of Living Beauty.

We are the expression of the Supreme Artist living from this natural state of mind, as the Child, as our Self. These enduring values are intrinsic to the mind and heart of each of us, including simplicity, gentleness, candor, faith, optimism, affection, teach-ableness, inner flexibility, far-vision, sweetness, being tenderly caring, fun, full of laughter and helpful. These are some of the natural qualities that exist forever between Creator and Created.

As the Child I can live in such richness without the need to possess anything at all. This is real. What a divine love affair we are having, Universe and I.

To find this eternal beauty which exceeds time and finite-ness, to live from the unbound fearless Soul, is to live again.

I need no more than this Love that has found me. Then it is my pleasure to give you my heart, give what I can, give to my world, give my Self to you.

Lovingly from your girl, always —

Love Always

You come to me as part of this wonderful Love I am. You are the one who comes to tell me of my ongoing beauty. You show me more of my Self. Here in this *earth-life* world, we find each other. The ones I love, they come into my life and shine here as a reflection of my own heart, my love. Their love shines in me, as I shine within them.

You are the reflection of my love. You are a sparkling gleam of light of my Self. You are me appearing to be you, a mirrored image of my own Heart.

The Soul of me is the life of me before I came into being. The little girl I am is an image of the eternal Self. Jesus said, "Let the little children come to me, and do not hinder them, for the kingdom of heaven belongs to such as these."

Love, human love and spiritual love, without love nothing would exist. Love is not something we do, it is something we are.

As I get closer, ever closer to my Self, I realize the subjective and objective become one. In my wholeness the world is seen as whole, holy and divine. Heaven and earth come together, the two become a single one. As the Child, I am wholeness *living*. I am solitary, elect and complete. Living from this childlike place we become fearless. Love is fearless.

Two
❦
Synergy

There is a synergistic thing that happens in the group. An idea emerges that the boldest dares barely to say. The lessor bold say, "Yeah." The bold and unbold bounce ideas off each other and suddenly something larger than the whole emerges. Synergy enables the less bold to do things they wouldn't do otherwise. The bold one who thinks of something doesn't necessarily have the nerve to put it into motion, but together they can do anything. The power of synergy takes over.

Synergy, it is real. I have found a synergy in my life. It lives and moves me. It is an energy, a magical solution combining this mystery of life and me.

Two little girls sitting on the floor trying to think what they will play next. One of them says something, the other says, "Yeah!" That's it. That's the synergy that is bigger than either of the girls alone. They start talking about the "yeah," adding bits and pieces to it, each sparking, lighting enthusiasm from the other. Finally, they know just exactly what they are going to start playing, and they do.

Together with nerve and verve, two people, a group of people, can put their ideas together and turn them into a synergistic force. It is real and things happen.

With this powerful force of synergy we are capable of putting anything into motion.

With you, my love, I felt it. There is a synergy that happens, it moves my soul into creative energy. Together we are untied, released, set free. The power lifts my soul and takes me flying over the fields and the valleys of time and space.

Out in the fields of imagination I find beauty merging and exploding.

We make love, you and I, soft tender mouth, sweet kisses, body to body, skin on skin, deeper yet, into the naked intensity of your soul. I am open, giving, we collide and the fervent heat blows us away.

Two become a union of magic and freedom that emerges out of this love.

Here in love, I am wide open to touch life. Life and I are deeply in love. I am both entwined and unbound, made free through this love.

Life and this untamed spirit of freedom, we are creating something to give. I give myself to this magnificent, wonderful existence. Why not?

I am filled now with this power, this synergy between life and my heart. I am riding life's rushing waves and sailing her deep ocean of Love. The synergy keeps me moving on. Pushes me, compels me. I am running barefoot again across the sandy beach, skipping, singing, dancing in pure, childlike freedom.

My heart has set sail and I have left the shore. Fearless, I fly, I roam, I move aimless and fearless through this world, through life, through my days alone, alone with the mystery and beauty of my beloved Light and Its sweet world.

I am having a love affair with *life*. The synergy of life and me and my soul combines. This synergy comes and awakens me. I am alive with its power. I am moved by the pounding force of life that fills me with wonder, curiosity and a desire. Desire that pushes me onward. The vital forces have transformed me. Youthful energy surges through me. My beauty is fresh and earthy and real. I will not rein this in. I will let it run free.

I am a child again, awake and ready to see what the day brings, what the next moment will be, what the future holds. I am indulging in the vibrant energy of this powerful pleasure of freedom. I am going where my heart wants to go.

And you, my love, and you – I love you always –

I found a balloon,
I think of you and let it fly away.

Writing

So, there I was on my porch in Aspen on that fall day in 1996. The sun was warm, the air cold, crisp and clear. Aspen is high in the mountains. At an elevation of 8,000 feet the sky is clear and boundless. The color of that heaven above was the deepest blue of blues. It was like sapphire blue and sparkled as such too.

The day was perfect. But Aspen days were always perfect. Fall was golden and bright. An icy breeze blew softly off the snow-capped peaks, causing those lovely orange and yellow dappled leaves on the aspen trees to spin, dance and twinkle in the shimmering sunlight. It was paradise. It was beauty and love expressed in ways that the senses, body, mind and soul, could feel it all.

Surrounded by the radiant beauty of the day, I began to read some of William's letters he'd sent me over the years. I had read them over again many times. I missed him and missed receiving his wonderful, surprising, prophetic, wise, funny, loving, honest letters since his passing. He used to send them rather frequently.

The letters in the box were unorganized. I thought to myself that one day I should put them in order as to the dates they were sent. I wouldn't do it that day, nor any day.

I pulled a letter out arbitrarily.

"June 10, 1986
"Dear Sandy,
"Keep up the work with words. Just the action of the writing process is a spiritual activity unrecognized by the world. Words are symbols of symbols. They are finite and man-made, yet, in the hands of an inspired story teller who knows what he or she doing they can do marvelous things in our wold. Can you imagine the world without the written word? Yet, the art of writing has only been around for a few millennia. Before that, the story teller was the shaman. The shaman was the story teller to whom everyone turned when they wanted to know something about the events over the mountain or across the river. Writing is still the same thing.

"Sandy, I love thee. Behind this human scene there is another Scene that is greater, higher, brighter, the substance of everything. That is the scene you're feeling and trying to write about. *Keep it up*, Lady of the Enchanted Cottage!

"Love from Billy at Woodsong"

Yes, he was so right, I was writing to him of the *Scene that is greater.* I was feeling the Infinite Light and Life that moves all things. I was touching, knowing this other dimension that is right here, right here behind the scene. I could touch and know the Substance that was being this world of matter and images. I wrote to him from the very heart and soul of me that knew Something greater. He saw that. He knew me. Even though, at the time, I didn't really realize how powerful and transformative this living light of perception truly was. I see it now. I know it now. I can share it now.

I write in abstract. I write in expressionist tones. I use my words to paint a lovely painting of a secret garden. I put my words on the page in order to bring a vision, an inner vision of this Sweet Light that stands behind this world of matter. I see the greater scene that stands here. I can combine metaphor, things I know and fantasy to create a message I want to share, to show you a place that cannot be seen except with the eyes of the heart.

I have been given a gift from the stars that I can know and see this other world that is here supporting all things. I am to share what I see as best I can. I write to the Heart of you, to the imagination, to the Soul. I write so you might be touched by my Love and see the deeper dimension that shines Its Light here as this tangible world we Live.

Return to Innocence

There is an alchemy that happens. We mix the two together, intellect and heart, mind and soul, ego and Identity, *what is* and *what is not*, objective and subjective, duality and non-duality. There, in this mixture, the Third appears. This is the alchemy of Love and the power of Light. Everything now turns into gold. The catalyst is Love. Love does the work. In the heart, matter and spirit become one, as the doors of perception are opened and the view becomes clear. I realize who I am, my identity and my world are the same. *Place* and *identity* are one. We cannot separate our identity from what we look out at and see around us. My *being* is what I see. Identity and place are one presence, one life, one knowing.

I am living in a new dimension as the Child. It's the same world but seen with new eyes, new mind, pure heart. The Child is raw and exposed and alive. The Child is fearless and open to feeling the inner delight of the holy spirit. The holy spirit fills my heart. The Child I am is my very own personal holy comforter. To me the return of the Child is the true meaning of "the second coming of Christ." It is joy, laughter, love and beauty, fully awakened to life. It feels like an angel comes to me, or perhaps a Tinker Belle of my own. She sprinkles me with cosmic glitter that sparkles in my soul. She scatters me with magic dust made of the timeless light of the starry nights and swirling planets at the edge of forever.

The divine holy place in me touches up close to this earthly, material life. The place of exchange is here within me. I feel the Living Presence. It moves me. It is me. My senses come alive. Everything feels alive. I am delighted by this as my physical senses have been awakened, aroused. I am pulsing with Life. The colors are felt and they vibrate and throb in a living beauty so deep. Textures, touch, the cool breeze on my skin, it's all luxurious and sweet and tender. God is Love and so am I. God is the energy of these sensuous feelings. The senses are acute to the sweetness of this living miracle of Life. I'm enraptured by the sights, the sounds, the music, the rain, song birds, green grass, the fragrance of your hair. God is Life and Life is sumptuous and luscious. I am the richness of this living Presence as the feelings, senses, sounds, touch, taste, aroma, soft kisses of your sweet lips, all moving me.

Stay with me and hold my hand my beautiful one.

Once upon a time, late one night in the quiet of those hours that sweet love woke me up to the music. He brought me songs and jet rides through my imagination. He untied my heart and my passion was freed. The love was rekindled. The flames began to burn in my soul. I came alive again. He was the out picturing of my own Heart intoxicated with love. I see it now. I see how it all works. It is magic. Now I can trust this world of mine. When we let go and feel the world, the world comes into us and feels us as well. Like two lovers in adoration of each other.

You came as the confirmation of this sensuous Light I found in my Self. You brought me the tangible evidence of this living, alive, feeling of life that I had uncovered in me. You came to my heart as the love in me. I love you. Do you know? Yes, I think you do. Genius that you are.

We have our glimpses. Then, sweet surprise, we find them in tangibility and then we can give them to our world. The glow of love is in my being and in my eyes. I am that love and I find that love in you, beautiful you.

Loving life from the heart of the Child is to know the light and beauty and the love of another. The light of these words is the same light as the Child you are. The alchemy of love and light happens between us and our world. This is the love I live that completes the interface between heaven and earth, between spirit and matter. This collaboration between us, between you and me, this was written before time. Divine destiny is working here. I know what I am to do, I know the power of the vision I see. I know what love is. I know we can and we will do what we are here to do. In the light of this love it will unfold to perfection.

Sweet world of mine. I give you my heart that you would find your heart always full and touched by God's ever-present bliss. I see the wholeness of your beauty and light, I see in you that which you see in me.

As a Child

Children are innately innocent, pure and good.

As a little girl I was often on my own, but I never felt alone. I enjoyed that no one kept tabs on me. Though of course, I was not responsible for myself. In fact I had everything I needed given to me. My life was quite perfect. I lacked nothing.

But, as a child, I still felt a sense of independence and self-reliance. I had very little supervision. There was no discipline and no rules.

What is so lovely is that I always did the right thing. I have always had this inner compass which points me to do good and be kind. I see how wise, tender and gentle my heart has always been. As most children are, I was imaginative and curious. I was full of boldness and audacity. I was also impetuous, filled with the desire to do things my way.

So that lack of parental oversight suited me fine. My childhood set me apart, at least in my little neighborhood where the other kids were bound by the set rules and limits their parents had put on them. I liked that I was not told what to do, but I did the right things anyway. Somehow all that freedom to make my own choices and my own mistakes has served me well.

I'd entertain myself with creative and imaginative ideas. I would think of some fun game to play and I would wander off finding ways to invest in my plan. Because I always enjoyed my own company I never really thought things should be otherwise.

One of the games I created was to leave little bouquets of wild flowers on a chosen neighbor's doorstep, then ring the doorbell and run. I wanted to do something fun, make someone happy, bring something sweet to those I didn't even really know and that was my nature.

Giving my Love to my world was inherent. As children the world is ours. Innocence and purity is all about love and giving.

It's about that thrill of seeing others happy and knowing you brought joy to them. It's about the feeling of happiness when others are happy. It's a sweet simplicity that holds the child's heart.

The profound truth now is that this unbound, joyful child of me is still here, alive and well. She didn't really go very far away, even in the passing years, when I thought she was lost from me forever.

Now, to my surprise, it's all come around again. I am this little girl, barefoot and bold with my heart right out here, vulnerable and tender and real.

I am open and willing to see what happens when I bring all my love to life, to others, to my sweet world. I want to see what happens when I leave a little bouquet of my love on the doorstep of my world. I want to place the wild flowers of my soul on the threshold of your heart. I want to see what happens when I give something of my soul, when I touch someone gently, deeply with love – when I ring the bell and run.

Memories of Summer Love

I was blessed to be a child living in a charming little beach town in Southern California. What a glorious place to be and such perfect times to be there.

I remember the joy of the ocean, the waves, the warm sun and the freedom of summer days.

The overcast of June skies would start to break sometime in the late morning. Sunshine would seep through the hazy grey. The clear blue sky would begin to emerge by noon. The clearing of the morning over-cast is almost instantaneous, as everything would turn suddenly bright and clear in minutes.

41

I would head for the beach, beach towel in hand, sandwich and cookies in a brown paper bag.

In the heat of the walk to the beach, the world sparkled as if lit with radiant rhinestones that covered the surface of all I could see. The cars parked, their slick shiny paint gleamed in reds, greens, silver, black, gold, shimmering flickering rays. I would watch the light on windshields flashing reflections of heat and bright radiant beams. The sidewalk twinkled like pavé diamonds. All the glitter everywhere was a world sparkling in my eyes.

I bounced and danced as I walked down to the beach, barefoot and sun-tanned, a child of the song. I was a little girl with strawberry-blond tangled hair moving to the rhythm of my happy heart and stepping in a joyfully anticipating pace.

Arriving at the cliffs, I viewed the vast, sparkling bright blue ocean. I would take the dusty dirt trail that led from the top down to the beach.

I had my own special spot in the sand where I would unfold my beach chair, a simple wooden set up with a green and yellow stripped canvas back. I could read, play cards with my friends, jump in the water, ride the waves, lie on the beach and soak up the sunshine. It was all mine. I would watch the ocean, listen to the soft sounds and feel the beauty for hours. I was in perfect peace there at the beach. I had everything and I felt completely free.

Living Both Views

"The Child and Its guidance are essential in our search. If one thinks his religion, his philosophy, or his theology is the means to finding the Final Answer, he is mistaken. The Child of Light and Love is the pathfinder, the guide, the way-shower up the mighty mountain... Science, religion and philosophy can take us a great distance, but the Child takes us to Dominion. It is absolutely essential that we actually get in touch with the eternal Child." —William Samuel

I have found the way-shower, the Child. It was a long road. As I grew into adulthood, life seemed to become a treacherous and scary road sometimes. I had lost my confidence in myself. But now I see it was a necessary road, a required road really, not actually treacherous at all.

Now I realize the sense of being invincible when we are young predominates, because at that young age we are still touching our childlikeness and the gift of the Eternal Self. The pristine, pure soul of our Self is the part of us that is closer to Reality, closer to the Truth. We feel invincible because when we are just entering adulthood we have not closed the door on our True Selfhood entirely. This Selfhood we know deep inside is immutable and omniscient. We are still open to that glimmer of Light wherein the higher vision tells us there is a living Truth and we are the very life and soul of this invincible Presence.

In the Light of Reality, these years down the road, it comes clear to me that indeed Life and I are invincible. I see Life is the eternal soul of me. Really, in the light of understanding, I see nothing that is Real is ever hurt. I see this Everlasting Life we are never dies. Our True Self, our Soul, our Identity as Awareness remains untouched by time-space-matter. Now I know in my heart *who I am* because I have seen, face to face, *what is real* and *what is not.*

I know this awareness I am is perfectly being whatever it is being. It is being *all that I am* because God is being all that is.

To Know for Sure

I am very sure of one thing, finding the Child started with faith. My faith told me that there is only one Divine Source that always was and always will be. Although that made sense to me, I still had to find out for myself if it was true. I had to make sure. I wanted to prove it. In order to prove it, I had to live it. I was not going to take anyone else's word for it. I had to find out, prove my heart's vision to be true or false.

Living this Divine Principle, the idea that *God is all that is*, meant I had to be brave, willing to trust my insights, my glimpses, my deepest senses of my heart and trust what Life seemed to be revealing to me. I had to test the *Oneness theory* like a scientist. I had to let go and live life just as if God is all, and that would be living like I naturally lived as a child.

Then, to my surprise, my test began to prove Itself to me, whether I'd wanted it or not. I was pushed into total willingness, having to let go and into self-surrender.

At that point of surrender, in that leap of faith, that is where I was given the way through and back to the Child/child again. That is where I found my way into this freedom. I was stripped, naked, raw, tender, vulnerable and alive again.

Yes, really, it all started on faith in the precept that God is all, total and only.

And I found out some things are true whether we believe them or not.

It was a winding road. I love to wander winding roads. I wanted to test this, to leap. And so, in answer to my quest Life provided the cliff.

I had to let go my old ideas of who I was. There was no choice if I were going to be honest. And honest I am. I gave up every belief I held dear. I had to, because my heart was torn wide open, I wandered the road, stood at the edge of the cliff and winds blew through me. There was no choice, all my beliefs spilled out and flew away, scattered into oblivion.

I had nothing to hold, yet there, right there where there was nothing to hold I touched Life Itself.

Here, in this openness and honesty, every untrue belief vanished with the powerful energy of my sincere desire to know. It swept through me and left me standing alone in purity and love.

Life came rushing in, as the dam was broken and the holy waters were freed to flow naturally down the river of my soul and through to the ocean of my mind. I was filled with Love's pure glory and freedom. I could not resist It. I knew I could only Live this Love that had found me now. I was free once again.

But to get here I wandered a narrow and steep path. I had to lose my confidence. Lose my beliefs, lose myself and lose my idea of God. I had to be brought down in order to rediscover and uncover my true Identity.

As I came to the top, I went through the gate that was only one Child wide. Alone, I had to enter alone. To my surprise and everlasting joy, I walked into the wide open fields of an infinite and glorious meadow.

Now Life holds me and shows me the secrets of the Child and the divine equation. The equation which is Living in the powerful and gentle rhythm with Tao, the Flow of this River, Life, the movement of giving and receiving. Here I am empty and full all at once.

We can repeat Lao-Tzu or quote *The Gospel of Thomas* or our favorite teacher or guru and whoever else we love, but one day we have to let go of even what they say and run free, barefoot and stripped of it all. Take it all off. Be vulnerable and touch It all by ourself. At least, that's how it was for me. I had to let go the teachings and find my own Heart without relying any longer on their words – eventually finding the Living One for myself. No one else between me and Life.

No words but my own mean the most to me – and that is as it should be for every one of us. Simple and so beautiful. It is all in your heart. The insight is yours. It comes to you alone. Live It.

This Light right here, this magic and love found me by way of my faith in myself. I trusted my way of seeing and understanding. I tested my own glimpses of the Truth and they proved true.

And yes, indeed, it started with faith *lived*. I was the brave one. Not knowing if I was right *first*. Not having anything to trust for certain, I had to live it; is God All? or Not? Now I embrace the world without fear or hesitation. My faith proved Me true. My teacher proved Me true. I proved Me true and God's Love proved Me true.

As I speak of myself here, I include all my heart, which is you and my sweet world, all of you. Trust who you are, trust your own Light. You know.

I love you, Sweet Love , thank you –

Riding Waves

Those days as a child come alive now in my memory, being young and happy in the summertime lying in the sun, warm skin glistening, slathered in cocoa butter. I can recall the scent of that cocoa butter even now, the very particular, strange but enticing chocolate-like scent. I am in a rapture of my senses.

Resting upon my beach towel on the warm sand, I drift in peace, fearless, whole and alive. A cool breeze is coming off the ocean. I hear the gulls calling over the waves rolling to shore. Lulled into dreamy peace, I am held gently by the soothing sounds of the sea, moving in and out. I hear the soft chatter of the pebbles rushing back and forth at the water's edge. All the sensuous sounds and feelings touch me like music.

Riding the perfect wave, joining it in sweet union, my body is lifted and taken by the cool green water. I feel its embrace as I let it hold me and take me.

Some days there are big waves. The sea is full of power and the breakers are nearly too big to ride. I swim out anyway.

One big wave after another. I'm diving deep beneath them. Beneath the waves is a holy sanctuary. I move down under the waves into a kind of sacred silence, underneath the turmoil of the crashing waves above me. Here, under the water, the sea sways me softly below waves and away from the breaking surf.

Beneath the waves I am alone. I am here with the gentle movement that holds me. It is so silent down below the surface. The deep water rocks me, easy, tenderly.

I am always enchanted by this mystical place under the waves.

Coming up for air, I see the perfect wave. I catch it. I ride it. It takes me all the way.

I ride another and another, salty and wet, my hair in tangled golden tendrils drip.

The hot sand holds my soft towel. My body chilled from the cold ocean nestles into the warm sand. The heat of the sand radiates and penetrates through me. I get closer, I snuggle into this hot earth beneath me.

A radio plays in the distance. Kids scream in delight. Laughter wafts sweetly through the cool sea breeze. The sound of the water, its crashing waves sing me into a dreamy land of infinity. I drift. I let go. I sail into oblivion. I am giving myself to this sweet love.

In time the sun gets low in the sky telling me the day is done. I hike up the steep, dusty path. At the top of the hill I stop and watch the ocean, the great expanse of sparkling Pacific waters bedecked with sailing boats gliding towards the harbor, on through the channel, going home at sunset.

All I see is an ever-present beauty. My heart is full. The sun is going down. Now the sky is turning orange, amber, pink and crimson, blues and gold, as I watch the horizon beyond the jetty.

My body, salty and tan, vital, young, barefoot and strong, can easily walk the few blocks to home.

I am in a neighborhood of charming beach cottages and lovely grand homes. Individuality and integrity emanate from each one. The care for these homes is obvious. Well loved, the little abodes are expressions of the owner's inner beauty and artistry. The houses seem to smile at me as I pass by.

Each home and yard is unique, special, with gardens full of roses and honey bees. I breathe in this sweet, fresh air so full of love. I feel this loving essence and a gentle joy carries me along. It leads this beautiful child's heart of mine sweetly up the hill.

A warm shower to wash the salty skin and hair. Sleep is heaven, sheets fresh and cool, the windows open, sounds of a nightingale and the distant hoot of an owl can be heard. The spicy menthol fragrance of the eucalyptus trees in the summer night's heat wafts into the room.

Life as a little girl is filled with all these sensory feelings. I am immersed in life touching me. This child is wide open to Life, vulnerable and full of eager anticipation for another day at the beach.

Upon sunrise, I awaken to expectations of a perfect day by the ocean, once more.

Time, remembering, dreaming of the past — yes, my love, there is no time. It's all here, right here, the love, the beauty, the song, here in my Mind, in my Heart, Living this Beauty and Truth always.

That little girl is alive and still here as the Life of Me.

I Love You —

Celestial Song

"There are two ways to live: You can live as if nothing is a miracle; or you can live as if Everything is a Miracle."
—Albert Einstein

My world is quite clearly nothing less than a miracle. It is the Uncaused Infinite Mind appearing in form. This is astounding, simply astounding. It is certainly a Living Miracle to me. It means *everything* is the nature of the Changeless, Immutable Isness of Something right here manifesting as my world. My world is made of the qualities and attributes of what is Eternal and Ever Present. Life is Living as Mind. There is nothing else here but this Infinite Illimitable Presence. God is the totality of all that is. Life and I are one, because there can be nothing outside of the Immeasurable One.

Life is simple and easy when seen and understood from the Child's awareness, the original Self. This is a familiar place. This is seeing the extraordinary in the commonplace of the world. This childlikeness I have found is so simple, so tender, It's myself. It is honest and down-to-earth in so many ways. We can live from our heart to see clearly and not worry about what to call It.

Now, I have nothing to lose and there is nothing to seek. Like the gambler I am, I open my heart, throw everything in, take a chance and let it ride. Something about me has become the wild cowgirl.

I can enjoy the whole magnificent beauty of this wonderful adventure, including the bumps, fast turns and the unexpected surprises.

Life is a joy. I can play now. Nothing but ongoing, eternal light and wonder dazzles my eyes, brings me laughter and lifts my feet off the ground. I can dance to this living melody of Life. I can feel the heartbeat of the universe. I am moved by the sounds of the infinite celestial symphony singing to me. I hear the music of the spheres. It rocks me, rocks my soul. There is a thundering energy in me now all the time. And there are moments when this vitality of love surges and I want to leap down the street in happy delight. And I do.

But, for now, baby, take me dancing tonight.

Ever since I turned into a butterfly I want to soar. Soaring, I am soaring through this soft sweet air of Life, through the breath of God, the sighs of lovers in love.

Or, maybe I am drifting away through the clouds in a hot-air balloon as the tethers have been let loose.

No, there is no difference now. God and this world are the same one. God and life and I are all the same sweet living light. I am the being and the seeing of God's eyes. I am not apart from God, so not apart from good, not apart from love. All I really know now is *this is it*, whatever *this is* that I have found. This did the job. I'll take it. This is good.

I see, be, live as this Divine Presence that is my world. This Presence is here being all that I am.

Where could I go, and what could I do that would or could take this Presence from me? No where, no place, not possible.

Amazing how things happen. To me, it's magic, there is no doubt. Everything, every moment is mystical and marvelous. There is so much energy filled with kindness and beauty here. It is too wonderful and It keeps coming.

There are friends, companions, my sweet lover, good people who come to help and give and love me. This flow of goodness and abundance never ends.

No, there is no guarantee, no insurance, no promises here for me. I live and Life continues to prove Its faithfulness to me. I have to live it without knowing where I'm going, because I don't know where I am going. I am naked and exposed. But I know that. I am willing to be open and vulnerable. It is the only way

50

now. I want to be here. I want to feel it all. I won't cover myself up. I won't rein my spirit in. I know my own beautiful heart. I know who I am and so I have nothing to fear.

Love Lives

On that sunny, brisk fall day there on my porch in Aspen I continued rereading William Samuel's old letters. It was lovely to have this box of correspondence. I felt fortunate that this man came into my life and gave me so much.

I was searching the words of each letter, looking for things I might have missed upon first readings, second readings, many readings. Searching for something he might have told me that I needed to know now. It seemed he saw something in me I didn't see at the time.

However, unbeknownst to me back then, in a few years I would know. I would come to find my genuine, authentic beauty, my sweet, funny, capricious, lovely Self, the Child. I would come to know a sweet Reality that would abide in my heart. I would come to know what love is and discover for myself all that this wise man foresaw. I would come to know that there is no paradox here. I would eventually find freedom, become fearless and live that gentle joy and Love again.

"Woodsong 1986
"Dear Sandy,
"There are many new things to write, Sandy. They all have to do with life and love, enthusiasm and childlikeness. They have to do with simplicity and tenderness, gentleness and the fact of Already. The new words have nothing to do with problems, or paradoxes, intellectualism or personality.

"Furthermore, they are difficult to write, they are difficult to say, because the old nature of us misconstrues, distorts and attempts to turn them into something ugly. So, I hesitate.

"The day is coming when these things will be listened to without so much askance and without such violent reaction. The fact is Reality is real, Reality is perfect, Reality is all. Transcendent Reality being all there is to the consciousness presently reading these words.

"One may say that at this moment consciousness seems to be filled with problems. But the believing that this is so merely gives authority to the seeming. We do not deny the seeming, we leave it, we let it alone and the power goes out of it. If the bird appears to eat a cricket, so what? Isness still Is, Perfection is still Perfect, All is still All, this Identity being us is still God's Self Identification and nothing we say or believe, or do not say, or fail to understand, can alter this Fact one iota.

"Strange as it may seem, there is a violent reaction within us when we finally get down to Reality Itself. You see, the old nature struggles vehemently to maintain its position. For most of us it requires a good stiff kick to alter our old opinions. But new light comes from the altered view, never from the old position.

"Sandy, you are a monumental and perfect you. Because perfection Itself is being all you are. There are many wonders in store for you and yours, as you go about the happy business of just being.

"Now, you are an artist, and you will know the wisdom of running off with the uninhibited, unbound feeling you see as Love. Now, it is tempered by the intellect, but Love is the leader. Hidden at the center of this feeling and barely noticed, is a sense of peace, tranquillity, serenity, a very gentle joy. It is the absence of elation the absence of discomfort. Oh but it is the transcendent presence of that which is being all sensation, all feeling. Now when you find this center, you will be delighted, for you will know that you have found another aspect of the Infinite Identity you are.

"This is the happiness that nothing can take from us. This is the Peace that does not ebb and flow between serenity and sadness.

"When next you ride up the valley where your special place is, rest for a time under one of your oaks, sit loose and feel whatever comes to be felt. Listen, listen to the heart and you will hear it and you will be refreshed.

"Who ever you think of at that time, think of love and feel the love you feel for that love is real and it is unbound and understands all things. God the Simple Truth is Love.

"Love is not fickle, love does not blow warm one day and cold the next, love is consistently Itself. Love, love looks and Lives. Love understands because love is understanding, love doesn't condemn itself or anyone else. Love is not guilty, love is not restrictive, it's not bound, it's not confined or contained, love is not beholden to any institution. All institutions exist by virtue of the fact that love Is, if indeed they exist at all. Love is not bound by the institution of marriage at all. It's silly for any of us, whether we appear to be in that institution or out of it, or a part of it or not a part of it, it is silly to believe that that institution is capable of providing us happiness or depriving us of happiness – It simply can't do it, not really, not when we see that Love, this Identity I am has the dominion.

"Love, there is only one Love, Love is love, it has no opposite. All Love is love, human love, personal love, sexual love, being in love, are all an aspect of infinite love which cannot be bound, cannot be circumscribed, cannot be confined, love, just simple love, whether we spell it with a capital letter or not, we mean the same Love, the very same Love, the very nature of being, the one that God is – the God that is Love, the Love that is Identity, here as I, as all.

"Singleness reveals the gentle Simplicity of singleness, the mysteries answered.

"I know what leads you, Sandy, and I trust you, you are important to us all.

"I love you, Billy at Woodsong"

The love and beauty in this letter settled like a seed in my heart and soul. It eventually bloomed and brought forth fruit.

Providence

That is exactly how it has happened for me, to me. Once I made my move, once I made the commitment to this idea that *God is all that is and is the very life I am,* well, providence moved in on me and took me by the hand.

That is how I found this deep abiding peace of mind and joy in my heart, or how It found me. That is exactly how it went; I had to believe first. I had to accept without proof that God, the Changeless One, really is *All That Is*. I had to live that faith and be the understanding that God is this Awareness I am. I had to trust that this Living Presence is the very Life I am. God's self-knowing awareness is aware – just the way I am. Nothing need be done to be more than what I already am. I saw it all clearly; I am not God, but God is the Life being all that I am.

Once I put my heart into that vision, made the commitment to be nothing other than God's very own Child just the way I am, imperfections and all, then all things came to my assistance.

I just simply began to be the little girl I once was, and be her totally and completely, to give her my all, to step out of the way and let Life have me. Then providence came along and brought all I needed in order to do what I needed to do.

Like a little gun-slinging Annie Oakley, I was going in, nothing was going to stop me. God was going to have to take me or leave me just as I am.

There were no sure bets, no nothing, only believing in my own crazy heart and soul that who I am, as this Child of God, is already fine by God. God was not asking me to be perfect before I entered the Kingdom. No, on the contrary, I was to enter as I was, flaws, sins, ego, unenlightened and all. God Loves this holy Self of myself. I lived It. I blindly trusted what I thought seemed true and took the actions of living from this purity and innocence of childlikeness that had found me. I was willing to trust this fully and totally. I was willing to get hurt and to be vulnerable and let Life do whatever it wanted to do to me.

Then, once I made that move, all things came to me and they continue to flow in my favor. Not that I would complain if it were otherwise. Not that I asked for things to go in my favor, they just did and they do. It's not about the results, it's about the joyful experience of existence. Some kind of Good pervades this providence. There is Good and Light and Love in all this.

Although, I would still be this immutable beauty I am even if things did not go well. It feels too wonderful and I don't really care how things go. I love being myself once again, and I love the freedom and joy of this transcendent unbound Self I am.

And furthermore, I will always say Life is good, no matter what the appearances. And I stand by that. It is the untroubled, effortless and fearless nature of this Christ-Light Child that makes it easy to live in the world no matter what appears to be. That is so good.

My very Self is my savior. I don't really care what happens, I have found the Messiah within me, in my heart. Here as the Child of me.

I could not have found freedom until I found my Self and now I know exactly who I am. That's where it all takes place, right here within me. It is a journey of Self-discovery. Self-realization, realizing I am the only one who can live my life.

A million sages gathered in the night could all stand pointing to the moon, but you alone are the only one who sees it.

I had to trust what my heart told me was true. I could not ever know for sure until I did it, until I lived out from the Heart that *did know* and from the transcendent Child's state of being. So I leaped. I reached for the gold ring. I found for myself that everything really is perfect – just the way it is. I only had to be what I already was.

Unleashed Beauty

Yes, the light and the passion and the love is too much to hold. This is extraordinary. This energy moves my soul and takes me up so high, and seems to thunder through me day and night.

The magic just keeps pouring forth and I have no room to hold it all. I just let it flow over me. There is nothing I can do but hold out my arms wide to this sweet love and let it wash down on me, like a child skipping in the rain, splashing in the puddles in her little red rain boots.

What I love so much is this *freedom* I feel once again. It is the freedom I felt as child. This heart of mine fills me with light and delight.

I am this unbound freedom, this unleashed beauty, vitality and effervescence. It does not come from me, it comes through me from the wide open spaces out there somewhere. Yet too, it is so close and so intimate and so much who I am, it is the Life of Me, my story, my way, my being.

And the most incredible thing is that this Life does not stop. It grows more beautiful every day – how is this possible? I watch it all unfold in its gentle and unrelenting Love. How did this happen? How did this Heart get so soft and easy, tender, real, alive, gentle, strong and wise – I don't know. I really don't know. I can only be it and breathe in this sweetness of Life and live It and give It. Give it all. It's all in the giving of my heart to you. I love you – that's just the way it is – and I smile.

A Story

A few years after high school, I realized a higher education was probably not going to work for me. I was intelligent enough to know the institution of education was not about the individual, not made for the rebel, or the artist. I knew my heart and soul wanted freedom, independence, creativity, and I had to do things my way. The school system had always felt like imprisonment to me. It was set up for those who wanted particular careers and I had no desire for a career. I saw the system as a dismal road to collectivism, a rut few can escape.

Besides, I had no use for what seemed to me wrong-headed group think. I liked being me and I didn't want to be indoctrinated or politically corrected.

Another asset, I was never one to feel sorry for myself. So I took my optimistic, positive soul and went my own way.

I always questioned authority. I was the complete antithesis of what education is designed for.

My temptation is always to break the rules and go off on my own adventure in my own way. I wanted to take a different path. I wanted the perennial questions answered. I wanted to know God and I didn't want the God of theology school.

Joseph Campbell often confirmed much of what I felt. He was one among my select few and best teachers. He had it right all along, "The purpose of every established religious institution is to PROTECT us from a god experience."

I didn't want to be protected, I wanted to know my own "god experience" first hand. I wanted freedom and then I wanted happiness. I wanted something genuine and honest from those who came into my life as teachers.

Yes, I wanted to learn. I loved to learn. I would do it on my own with books I chose, with nature, with life, with my favorite philosophers and the very special works and writings of spiritual teachers that resonated with me. I wanted the freedom to follow my own heart.

As Sweet Life Is – Destiny unfolds –

My Sweet Rocky Mountain High

As I was wandering the winding roads, eventually I followed a path that led me to Aspen, Colorado.

Aspen was, back then, a rough and tumble little ski town full of wonderful eccentric and adventuresome people. Such a great town. There were the ski bums, cowboys, farmers and hippies, savvy businessmen, artists, intellectuals and philosophers, outdoorsmen, hunters, climbers, sophisticates and musicians. What a bountiful world it was. What a pleasure of sights and sounds and expressions I got to enjoy.

Skiing, playing, working, Aspen was fast paced with a nice clarity about it. It was a perfect place for keeping up with the pace and learning to be myself. The energy of the mountains was very good for my soul.

There in those glorious mountains, nature was the panacea, the healing balm my soul desired. The peaceful feeling of being outside in the splendor of so much natural beauty was what I loved.

The tranquil, deepest blue of the sky, the clouds, the gentle breeze kissing the aspen leaves that shiver and spin in the icy, clear mountain air was pure beauty. Beauty was essential to me. The changing seasons were incredibly exquisite. The summers were green and cool, fresh and sweet. The fall was bright and crisp drenched in the colors and light of yellow, ambers and golden. It was clear and blue there, the beauty was everywhere I looked and it all just moved my soul. My mind, my heart, my spirit was filled with that radiant glorious beauty and I thrived on that peaceful beauty.

Winter would bring a softness, a holy silence even though there was the commotion of skiers, tourists, and working in the fast pace of my little jobs that helped to pay the rent.

Springtime, of course, brought the buds' flowers and the cottonwoods would come alive. The lilac trees would bloom and the sweet first glimmers of green unfolded, turning everything into the magical landscapes of a grassy, leafy emerald city.

Every season felt like a sweet hallelujah. Each season a gift of its own expression. Life has been good to me. My heart was good, my soul was good. I was good. I had plenty of the kind of peace and quiet I loved, while also being out and busy, keeping up with life around me. I was starting to break free again. Gain my self-assuredness back. I was beginning to breathe again.

I was awakening to the Truth at a deeper level. Slowly it unfolded. The Light of my own heart was taking care of me. I was sensing a divine peace in my heart and in my life. I was coming to know that I am not only this sense of being a separate person in an objective world, but I am a part of the Infinite Presence being the wholeness and entire realm of life. Intellectually, I could see that I was really the entire whole of everything that is, the entire cosmos, in fact, the universe. These ideas eased my soul.

I could trust the insights that were coming to me. I had glimmers and glimpses that the universe is the very Presence of God. God is all that is. I was seeing that everything is sacred and perfect just the way it is. I didn't need to change myself, I only needed to understand. I was seeing it all in the light of a sweet simplicity that was becoming very clear. I would write about my latest insight, work it out in words, on paper. I would write and think about how Life and I are one, how everyone and everything is my Self. I could see how Life was entwined with me.

I considered how I was Life Itself, the tangible evidence of God's infinite presence, and everything is as it should be. I started to live that idea and trust Life again. I was learning and discovering and testing myself. I knew there was a bright, light and charming, funny girl in my soul, I knew I had put her away and I wanted her back.

Things were going well in that little town. It was paradise. I belonged there.

The White Kitchen

Back then, back in the days when I first got to Aspen, I had a little job as a waitress. I remember my early morning treks though town. I would be heading out to work the early shift. Stepping out into dark, it must have been around 5 A.M. I was dressed warm and took out on foot across the silent town. The sky above was still inky black, but there was a distant heavenly glow at the edges of the mountain tops. The light was like a soft celestial, angelic halo that touched the rim of the high peaks as daylight of morning was nearing. At that altitude the stars are so bright it is as if they could be touched. In the cold and dark hour, the radiant, twinkling sky was a beauty to behold. So silent out there at that quiet time. Walking alone under the night sky, I felt I was being looked upon by heaven's cosmic wonders, the Big Dipper, the Seven Sisters, all so close. Venus, Mars and Jupiter were dazzling me in the infinite darkness.

I loved my early morning walks. There was a deep, holy stillness that touched my soul. Only the crunch of the snowy road under my boots could be heard. The air was fresh, icy, dry and crisp. My breath was visible as it hit the freezing air. I was full of happiness and wonder, invigorated being outside in the magical feel of that still of the night.

I was treading through the streets, wearing my hat, mittens, a turtleneck, corduroy pants and pink lightweight wool sweater. Decked in the style of a mountain girl, I could not be without my waist-length, green, Gerry-down ski parka, along with my little blue canvas backpack slung over my shoulders. I was carrying my skis and boots in hopes to get a few runs in after work.

Coming into the down town, it was still dark out, I entered the little cafe. The silence was broken as I walked in. It was warm inside. I was embraced by the warmth and charmed by the bustle of noise, clanking dishes, the men talking. It all contrasted suddenly with the pristine, silent, long walk I'd taken to get there.

Activity, commotion, laughter, smiles, cheers of good morning hellos would be coming at me, "Hey, Sandy's here!" "Good morning, we've been waiting for you!"

The grill was sizzling, eggs and bacon, pancakes whipped, dripped and flipped. Wafting aromas of breakfast and hot coffee. I was delighted how the truck drivers and lift operators would light up when I walked in.

I put my apron on. I brought the hot coffee. I made them smile. We bantered and they cracked jokes. I would pour them refills. They would tease and flirt with me. I enjoyed it.

The White Kitchen was the only place open at that time of morning. It felt safe and happy there, cozy and welcoming. I liked that job. I enjoyed the sense of authenticity. It was a place for the working people, the trash-men, the snow plow guys, the lift operators. And they all knew each other. I liked the sense of being among friends and feeling at home.

It was a small cafe in the middle of town, wedged between the Paragon and Delice Pastry. The single counter faced the grill and it sat about eight people only. The boss and his wife would always be in a hurry, moving fast, always hard-working people. They ran the place by themselves. We were often very busy keeping the local regulars fed and happy. It was a good place to be on a cold winter day. The heat and activity inside created lots of energy steaming up the front windows. I enjoyed that job for those few winter months.

In those days, working for a business in town, we would get discounts on our lift tickets. With the employee pass it cost me only a few dollars a day to ski on Aspen Mountain.

After my shift, skis in hand, I would head across the streets over to the lifts. I could catch a few runs down snowy-white Ajax before the day was done.

Things

Some scientists tell us that everything is made of vibration, moving information, particles and waves. Thoughts, ideas, words, dreams, imaginings, the tangible and intangible are all vibrations.

Vibrations are words, so perhaps this is something about the Bible verse, "In the beginning was the Word, and the Word was with God, and the Word was God."

From what I have gleaned, I am living in and as this realm of symbols. The formless Mind of God is seen in form as God's

62

qualities and attributes, witnessed as this profuse expression of the appearance of tangibility. This universe is the Infinite Mind appearing as this objective, solid world – like words, symbols, just like the Word. A changeless Divine Principle stands ever here behind the appearances, the symbols. The symbols come and go, but the Eternal Source will forever be the Living One.

I realize that the world is speaking to me as if every *thing* is metaphor, a symbol, full of meaning and information. Or I could say time-space-matter is *idea* made visible-tangible.

This is the ever present world of synchronicity. Life is a story based on a Divine Principle. We are living the symbols that teach us what is already known and unfolding in time. We are living the *living word* of God. We are the breath of expression of one beautiful Divine Mind. The world is the manifest existence of God's consciousness. It is me. I am It, light flowing forth Its electrical sparks of information.

Well that all sounds strange and rich and so it is. Living a living metaphor amazes me and keeps my soul ablaze with the feelings of mystery. Life is profound and wondrous.

My happiness is easy now. I need nothing to make me happy. I am the living Child, the wellspring is within me.

I'm reading the story here by the night's light of the silvery moon. I am thinking of you, my love. I am enjoying finding the clues, listening to the marvelous tale of a wonderful adventure. I'm wondering, with the anticipation of a child listening to mother read a fairytale. I am enthralled with life, waiting to know how each chapter will go, where it's all leading. Tell me the story. Let's read some more and see where they go tonight.

Reincarnation Returns

I believe in reincarnation. I know I have lived previous life-times. In some strange way I just know – nothing I can explain. I can recall some of those lifetimes. I recall the stories. Vivid ones. Real to me. They sing deep in my heart. I remember them. And I remember you, my love. You were the wounded knight taken into the monastery to heal. I, the holy woman of God tending your wounds. The Love between us, the unbridled nature of our passion unloosed. I remember. I gave myself to you. I was enrap-tured by your soul, your beautiful heart, your goodness, your eyes, your warmth, your loving desires seeking my comforting places.

Now, in this life, an old love is re-found. Mysterious and beautiful how Life powerfully moves us toward each other. We collide at the same place, the same time, and a connection like electric happens. This is sweet serendipity. I feel that magnetic pull, that powerful chemistry. I am drawn toward a rare few. The attraction moves us, and it all overflows in the earthy pull of our passion. We overlap from life to life. I have been here before. I know you. A deep memory stirs, and I recall who I was. Yes, there is no doubt that I know you. We melt sweetly into each other. Easily, exquisite feelings of a holy Love coming into me. We have always known each other. You, sweet prince of the kingdom, shining hero of Love – and well – I know, I know we have been together always. Life is Sweet.

Three

Overtone

Even as I write my story, all these years later, I still find new meaning and glimmers in William's letters. All this time down the road, I find more synchronicity and confirmation here in his words.

I also know this Child leads me always. The Child has led me through this world all along, even when I didn't realize it. The Child has taken me through the labyrinth and across the narrow pathway to the mountain top. The Child brings the learning of whatever it is I might need to know now. My heart is prepared for the days ahead. I thank all that has led me here.

This prophetic letter William sent to me is from his private unpublished journals.

"Private Journals 5/26/85

"Most of the people who have 'been given to me' have been students of metaphysics – and their instruction has been woeful. It has seemed wise to tell them how to get their subjectivism straight. But, beyond that, I have been given the role to teach the teachers for the days ahead. Not one out of a hundred has really heard me. Not two in ten thousand. But now, the future teachers are *assembling* to lead the way through the troubles to come and to be Lights to the world at that time. This work is for them, and for the Children of the world who will come alive in them."

Yes, those of us who have learned from William's work, those of us who have found the unbound freedom of the Child one way or another, we will find the way to Light the path for others in these days to come.

Finding the Child is finding the one real and only authority within, "closer than fingers and toes." With this Self discovery we realize there is no need for leaders and followers.

We tell others about this marvelous essence of Light that leads us. It all becomes easy. We move along with Life's sweet and powerful song. We no longer seek reliance on external authority. We hear another sound and it sings in our heart.

To discover the inner way-shower is to find real freedom. We live this freedom. We are not beholden to false authorities, established systems, doctrines, hierarchy and dogmatism.

If the teacher has found this Divine Child they most certainly will not keep this Light hidden. They will teach of this Living One that abides in the heart of everyone. They won't hesitate to shine their Light telling others of this Holy Child within.

Here, as the Child, we find the unbound joy, and the gifts, the ways and abilities to share our Light in our own individually expressed, fearless and deeply touching way.

Truth is written in your heart. As this Living Light, we are no longer subject to fear, therefore, no longer reliant on external authority and false security. We have found the Living Waters of Understanding.

The days ahead are now upon us. It's time to run with it.

Cosmic Child

The sweet, enchanting, cosmic Child I was when I was little girl, she has come back to me. She speaks to me now, telling me about *the time before time*. She is my original Self. She is the one who lives on both sides of time and space.

She isn't afraid to speak her unorthodox and exuberant words now. She is ungoverned and ungovernable. She is the golden point, that perfect balance, strong and steady, honest, bright and the closest thing to God. She is real, and she is smart, instinctive, funny, bold. She doesn't mind the gravel and bumps along the road of life because she knows it is often the friction that drives things forward and keeps us moving along.

She is like the photon, made of illimitable light, unrestricted and instantaneously everywhere. She is the wave, the particle, both and more than either. She is the Presence that includes all that is, right here and right now.

She knows things I do not know. She takes care of me here in the world. Like a guardian angel, she helps me make the trip through time and space. She makes it sweet and easy. She eases it all. She knows the way. She knows the Truth. She is my twin Self. She loves me as herself. I love her as mine. Devoted to her as she is to me.

This Child sits next to Reality, which brings me great joy to know. I love how audacious and free she is. She loves to love. She lives on the unseen side of this world and holds my hand on this side. She shows me what I need to do here in the world. And I am very capable of doing it.

This twin Self of me is Reality come alive. Actually she is more Real than anything I could ever be. I could not have lived my liberation had she not found me, returned to me, given me the courage and done this with me.

Since I have found her again, I see now these days in my life are just the beginning. I have walked through a door into a new world. I have been shown an open Meadow.

Come on, sweet love, run with me now. We can explore this limitless beauty of Life. You are free and I am free. I am, most of all, fearless and in love. I really don't need to know more than this. I don't need any more than this. I have put the search down. Flying now, soaring, nothing holds me down.

I can watch the glory of this Meadow blooming right before my very eyes. Life has become magical. This is the Shekinah, the holy ground. This place is sweet, divine, lusty and alive.

Remarkable. Divine Intelligence Itself has brought me to this innocent heart of mine and I am not turning back.

I am this unending awareness expanding through other heavens to traverse. There are more stories to be told, more life to be explored, more gentle glens and rough roads all right here in this ongoing world of mystery and love.

Uncharted Wilderness

This lover of mine gives me free rein. I'm unleashed. I can take it or leave it.

I'll take it. I like what we have. I like this.

I have no reason not to venture here where my magical spirit has led me. How could I refuse my own beauty's temptings as I am presented such an arousing gift of Love.

This Love says come, follow me, come with me. I can't resist the call. Like a bird that feels the urge to fly south, it is innate in me, I must go where this goes.

I'm on the back of a speeding motorcycle. We're on a mountain road. I'm holding on to him, tight, my face nuzzled against his black leather jacket. I breathe in the scent of the warm leather mixed with the sweet, comforting heat of his body.

I keep my eyes closed. We are moving fast. I trust him. I can't see what is coming. This takes being vulnerable, open, so I can feel the movements within me, lean into the swift turns on these curving, twisting roads we ride.

I'm the fearless elation of immeasurable trust. I'm the eager excitement of the roll of the dice. I cannot predict which way we will go. I ride easy, I let myself feel this beauty and power that rushes through me.

I hold on and let go at the same time.

This is a *joyride*.

This is love and freedom unleashed and I feel it all. I'll take what comes. I'll give in to the unknown.

This beautiful, tender heart of mine is filled with purity and faith. God is Love and yes, so am I. I hear this sweet, soft laughter inside me as I realize how strange and wonderful it all is.

I'm so surprised I am here. Surprise – this wild, frolicking, delightful energy comes to me now, again, once again.

Yes, I'll take this voyage, with only the stars in my eyes as my compass.

I see no reason not to.

My soul would not and could not pass up this delectable meeting with kismet. I have been brought here into this uncharted wilderness. I cannot turn down what was written before time. I must ride it all the way.

I'll accept this love that has found me. I'll receive this sacred gift, letting It come into me. Impregnated by the Beauty, I give birth to new worlds.

My heart, my love –

For God's Sake Dear — The Mystic

William sent me a few articles on mystics and what they were. He told me mysticism is the opposite of reason. He told me I live from the heart and that I am a mystic. In the articles he enclosed, it said the mystic experiences "powerful forces that lift them out of themselves."

The mystic "has a knowledge, an experience which is never entirely separable from union with God by way of love." And George Santayana observed, "The mystic smiles at science and plays with theology, undermining both." C.S. Lewis's phrase for grace is "surprised by joy." The article continued, "As Shelly instructs, 'Let us recollect our sensations as children.'" And furthermore, to my delight, it says, "The mystic feels a deep and profound peace, has a sense of joy and laughter, is filled with a certainty that all things will work out for good. The mystic has a high level of mental health and the mystic has a conviction that love is at the center of everything."

The genuine mystic is the simple, trustworthy, holy Child. There is a Child in us that sees the Child in everyone. The Child laughs, the Child sees beauty, the Child plays games, the Child is honest, the Child is real, and the Child is eternal. The real fact is the Child is the whole of us, the real of us and of everyone.

The articles' declarations or not, it's evident to me I have been transformed. I am the unconstrained Child. I experience God firsthand, directly. I am truly "surprised by this joy" that found me, and I certainly did nothing to deserve it.

The Child knows the real. Only the Child of us knows the wheat from the tares. And only the Child of us has the courage to leave the tares alone until the harvest.

I was asked what my book is about. The questioner looked curious and delighted when I told them the book is a love story.

I went on to say that my writing is an expression of unbound joy and wonder from a little girl who is dancing to the music of her soul. I can't help but to put words to the song in my heart. Like breathing, I just do it.

The doors to a new perception have opened. Something was unloosed in me. Something in me walked into the wide open frontier.

It surprised me how full of whimsy, beauty, sensations and divine wisdom my spirit and my world has become. And I am one living joyous contradiction. I am just fine with all this. It is who I am. This is my true Self rediscovered. Not what I thought I would find. But indeed what I am. I'm enjoying my freedom in this new, yet ever so familiar and sacred state of mind and heart.

So pleased that I cannot be and won't be pinned down or held to any convictions or ideologies.

As an artist and a lover, and lover of God's Love, I have to express this – like a bird has to sing, or as an apple tree bears fruit. It just happens in the DNA or something.

Here too is the amazement of it all. I watch as this unbound Spirit leads me, brings me whatever I need in order to do what I am doing. I trust my Self and Life. I've been the witness of this magic unfolding within me. It is clear to me. There is no denying a transforming light of beauty and youth has come into me. I am full and lifted up to the wholeness of *my being.*

I want to play in the rain with you. I love to dance in the rain. Come with me, let's dance here where the wind is wild and the trees are blowing sideways in the storm.

I have spiraled upward and out. I feel an energy that moves through me. It is powerful. It is strong, unconcerned and carefree as it bubbles into my world.

I'm running through a field of wild flowers now. I can enjoy the open fields with you. Hold my hand and come run with me.

The enthusiasm goes unabated as this illimitable beauty cannot be contained. Uninhibited and unrestrained, my spirit is beyond time and matter.

I have become a butterfly and dusty drops of yellow pollen are falling from my wings as I fly.

This is mine to give. I give my heart, my words, my love to my world – I have to.

"As it might be said in the East, the night of Brahman falls as soon as the harvest of the Seed is accomplished. The Morning of the New Day comes quickly."

As long as forever my love –

Everything Is Ego

"The world is sacred, a perfect vessel. It cannot be improved. If you tamper with it, you will ruin it. If you treat it like an object, you will lose it." –Lao-Tzu

Exactly what I love, everything. I Love everything. I am absolutely undone and running free.

I don't have to pull life apart into ego and not-ego. That's not even possible. It can't be done. There is nothing but ego. Life is ego. Life and Identity are inseparable. Life is this Self-knowing-identity I am. Life is one big ego trip and I am going to enjoy the journey.

I am simply Living the wholeness and allness of everything I am. It is about love. Love makes no demands. Love asks nothing of me. Love lets me do it my way.

This endearing place I know, this place I have found, it's all-encompassing, including me and you. Nothing is left out of this Wonderland of Being.

And to Love others, that is the real Joy.

You my love are here, as I am here. What can be outside of Life? Not a thing, not ever. I'm letting it all in with arms wide open.

Funny thing, as I let it all in, as I embrace Life, It embraces me back. It returns the Love multiplied exponentially.

God and I, Life Itself, the very soul of me, the light of my heart, we are deeply in love. I'll let it Love me. As I am cherished by Life, I discover I am cherished by you. Of course. I am in love and I am safe in the arms of this Lover, the Divine Presence that cares for me sometimes appears here, as you, my love.

I have been led to this Meadow of sweet bliss and tender kisses, where soft pink rose petals fall from my eyes. I am waiting for you to come home. You bring me flowers, a bottle of fine wine, the evening is spent in your strong and gentle arms.

I'm doing that. I am resting in the calming green grass with you. We are laying under the wide blue sky and watching the clouds float by. I am kissing your fingers as you hold my hand. We drift with the clouds and breeze and the little song birds chirping in the trees. I hear the gentle stream as its icy waters move past us.

The doors were opened, the new day arrives, it is a bright shining day. It shines here in my heart. You are here in my heart. Life is here in my heart. It's all here in my heart.

I'm open to it all, to live here in this passion that goes to the depth. It is pure and holy here with you, my beloved one. The fearless power that I have discovered is my own Soul. My Soul includes pale-pink rose petals and the light in your lovely eyes.

There is a portal within this heart of mine – which is really the world of mine – a portal between heaven and earth. I will indulge in this blessed reverence I feel for this precious surprise. I can't refuse this Love. The angels and the gods have invited me to such a wonderful party. I am feeling an expanding abundance of form and tangibility as the magic takes shape.

Yes, I love you –

Ego Again

I did not need to get rid of my ego, that is for certain. No, actually the real joy and fearless freedom came to me when I realized I get to keep my ego, that I cannot separate ego from Life. I am the most essential part of the whole blissful equation. My ego is the one Life lives. Life is my ego lived. Life. Life is known by me, with me, through me, as me. Where is Life without me?

Clearly the presence of Life and my sense of my identity are connected. Clearly, wherever I go, I am still here, still present. Somehow presence and who I am are one coexisting experience. When I go somewhere I am always present wherever I am. That's not just poetic, it is a fact. In some ways, I go nowhere really. *Who I am* and *where I be* are one in the same. Place and Identity are one. I am and Life is. Life and I are one, always here. Here is always where I am. I could travel to the ends of the earth and I would not have left *here* nor *myself* behind. I am Life being. As one, there is nothing between us. Ego is Life and Life is who and what I am. Life is always here. How amazing it all is. And how marvelous this ever-present, all-inclusive world of my Self is. I love it all, and I love you.

We begin to love our world again. We see that this tangible world cannot be separate from the Spiritual Light that is being all this. If I deny myself the goodness, the beauty and joy of this cup of coffee right here in front of me, then how could I expect to see the superlative Good *being* the cup of coffee? Clearly, to love my tangible world is to Love God too. It is certain, now so clear to me, the two are one. I will not deny my sweet, tender, simple human good feelings, no, I will enjoy them in the fullness of the miracle they are. I am touched by the simple, everyday wonders of the little things, the extraordinary in the ordinary, and that feeling opens my heart to the Superlative Love/Good that is here standing behind Everything.

Yes, God is good. His mercy is everlasting. His blessings are here and everywhere for anyone and everyone. The peace "that passeth understanding" can happen at any time. In a moment, when we see the beauty, the ordinary miracles of every day, the peace can break right through. And with the Child, yes, with the Child it does. This is a mystery.

All Within the Heart

"And I shall write my law in their inward parts and write it in their heart; and will be their God, and they shall be my people. They shall teach no more everyman his neighbor and every man his brother, saying 'Know the Lord' for they shall all know me from the least of them unto the greatest of them, saith the Lord, and I will remember their sin no more." –(Jeremiah)

It was all a matter of strange twists and turns, unexpected and sometimes unwanted.

On my way to seek the Truth, Something Divine has found me. This was not the enlightenment I had in mind. So simple, so amazing, this is nothing like what I was expecting to find.

I'm not sure what I did to get here, or what this is. It feels like grace. It feels unearned and undeserved. It is the sweetest surprise of all. I was given a ticket into some new world. Oh, yes, such a beautiful world. I've been lifted up into a truly magic kingdom. I don't know how it happened, it just happened.

I didn't really know where I was going, but here I am. Something seemed to shift ever so slightly, ease into view, coalesce, and I became whole, alive and very happy. Wherever I am, it's someplace that I like.

Oh yes, I always believed and I always had faith, and I always looked up and out and into the distance, seeing life from a very wide-angle lens of my mind, trusting Life, anticipating good things. I did seem to see life from a third eye, as I always kept my vision on those higher ideals, despite how things may have looked or seemed.

Now I have returned to a sweet place. It is a new land and yet such a sweet and familiar place. I am home really.

I feel like I've come back to where I began but nothing is the same.

I think now I'm simply here in this world to Love. To Love because I cannot Live any other way. Love is the reason I live. Love is the only reason I am here. I know Love is really all that matters.

Giving my heart is irresistible. Giving my heart to my world, that feels so good. And I love being in love with my lover. My lover is simply irresistible to me. I live this new light as it comes to me to live. I cannot do otherwise now.

I know this sweet state of my soul is a holy gift.

Finding my freedom is such an unexpected surprise to me. I really had no idea how beautiful this would be. The fields of wild flowers are growing fuller as I watch it all unfold before me.

I only know I have found an abiding peace of mind that shines in radiant gleams of light right here in my heart, always.

Really, nothing stood in my way, ever. Nothing. But I had to find that out by myself. I had to make that discovery for myself, so this would be mine, personally, tenderly, completely mine, that I would really know it for myself.

This is freedom. This is the unbound joy I wanted. This is simplicity, tenderness, without purpose or agenda. It turns out to be such simplicity. This peace is a heartfelt lightness of living, a flowing, moving and doing. I can't help it. I am bursting with a joyful song and want to sing this song that is in my heart.

I am filled with enthusiasm and wonder and delight. I don't mind putting it all out here and letting you have what I can give. I don't mind what happens now. I know how wonderful and real this transcendent freedom is. It is immutable, no matter what seems, or what appears to be.

I've never been reticent to disobey the rules. You set a rule and I'll look for the way to break it.

I have always been a rebel, all my life.

Maybe it was this rebel in me that led me to find this wild, wide open playground I freely romp now.

I wanted freedom and I challenged the status quo. I never accepted what I was told. I had to find out for myself. I love my curious, daring nature. Children are curious and daring.

I love Life mightily. The more fearless I have become the more Life touches every particle and cell of me. I have a vitality and joy and ease with everything.

Now, I breathe it deep. I see the heart, the soul, the beauty behind everything and everyone. I love this.

Slowly, precept upon precept, I was filled with a sense of the Divine Presence, everywhere. I see it. It's here. It's all there is.

Despite the bumps and sharp turns that might come along, the ride is pure magic. Life is kind of like the old Mr. Toad's Wild Ride at Disneyland. I climb in my little cart and I ride. The crazy scenes fly by me and I know nothing can hurt the Light of this Self I am. It's all powerless and harmless. I am full of little girl giggles and joy. I can enjoy this ride.

Brave Leaping

Though I was led to the edge slowly and did not know I was coming to the edge, eventually I was at the edge.

I remember the day of the final leap. I remember the leap. I remember I could choose to turn back. I had a choice. I could turn away, not leap. I had reached the Rubicon. I remember the feeling that if I did not do it now, my chance would not come again. I knew what I had to do. So, I leaped.

William once asked, "Where are the brave?" And I stood up. I would be the brave.

Yes, it is about the brave. That's really it. That's how this Love all came flooding into me. I was brave and I trusted my own Heart – and I leapt.

I was surrendered. I was unloosed. I was released. I was let go. And unleashed, I began to fly.

I had the audacity to go against the tide. I was not afraid to die so I figured I would dare something that could be a mistake and might kill me. What did I have to lose? I could see it made no difference. It mattered not what happened.

I had the passion and desire to give my life to see for myself. No one could live my freedom, my life, my light for me, but me.

This heart of mine busted out and broke the rules and made its way into the open fields, into the sweet joy of the meadow.

I am free, and I am back to where I began.

But this time it is a new world, it is a new place entirely. I *know* that I know. That makes everything new. I am in love again. Deeply in love. I am flowing in this ongoing action of Life. Everything comes to me, and keeps pouring in and flowing out – and yes, all for me. Does this sound self-centered? In many ways it is. It is the only way really.

The one I love is in love with me. My Sweet, divine Life is my Lover. I love my world and I love you.

I know my soul. I know who I am. I live this sweet, uninhibited, unrestricted knowing without restraint or hesitations. I abide in a tender place, a patient place, whole and holy. It is a feeling of genuine kindness, it is honest and gentle and strong. It is the Presence I have found and it has made me fearless and bold and brought me peace.

My whole world flows through me now.

It's not about preserving my world, insurance and control. It's not about what happens. It's not about being safe, or getting anything, or having things go my way. But yet my world is filled with more glory and wonder, preservation, security, goodness, riches and creativity and everything I want and need than ever before.

The world that seems to be out there is really me, it is my Self and it is mine.

Everything is about me. It is all about my feelings, my thoughts, my imagination, my soul, my attitude, my outlook, my state of mind. It's all about me – just as it is all about you. There is one Self-awareness here. It is infinite and all. It is who I am. It is about my bold and beautiful heart. Everything and everyone is included in this unbound heart of mine.

Yes, this *everything* that is about *me* is the same *everything,* the same I and me and mine and Life as you are, as yours, as yourself, the all-inclusive awareness you are. Here, expressing as you, expressing as me. As Catherine of Sienna said, "My me is God.... Nor do I see any other me but my God himself."

The joy of being you and me. The unbound joy of being Life Itself while also being special, unique, individual. There is only one you, and only one me, and there won't ever be another like you. Not another like me. Sweet Life.

Oh, and that's why I love you –

Anticipate New Light

There in my Aspen home, I unfolded another letter I had picked randomly from my treasure box.

In this letter William wanted me to understand that finding this honest clarity in my own heart does not necessarily protect me from the harsh actions and cruel words of others. He was wise to warn me. Yet too, as he says, this tenderness of heart is beyond intimidation. The Child laughs in delight and takes nothing personally. And yes, yes, I am finding more wonders and uncovering more secrets than I might imagine. The glimpses continue, to my genuine amazement.

"Woodsong on the Hill 6/17/85

"Tender Sandy, new child of Seven Days. I send this letter from New Zealand to show you how far your words have gone and what respect they created. You might also glimpse a bit of the awful vitriol and toxicity I am subjected to even when my intentions were only good – how the world misperceives, misconstrues and attacks the most innocent of us, never realizing the Gift. Previews of coming attractions for you – because you shall be a Revealer too.

"I took the liberty of writing your mother an apology for asking her that question that perplexed her so. You perceived in part why the question. Slowly and surely, you and the Child of yourself will catch the other half of the Equation. I'll know when you find that too! And you and I will be together even more closely – in unexpected moments – in even GRANDER ways. Watch and see!

"Thank you for all the inner delights you are, my Sandy. Thank you for feeling Love so immaculately and warmly. I love you, new lady.

"Be still. Be quiet. ANTICIPATE new light and Love. Be wise to whom you tell of your inmost wonder! Delight in those grand feelings and I will too, with you.

"You have many important things to do in the world. Please take my word for that! You've trusted me this far, so I want you to believe the rest as well — MORE wonders than you might imagine.

"Please write to me as you feel disposed to. Do you keep a private journal of your Glimpses? You must. Ask why if you wonder. I don't remember if we've talked of that or not. Learn my secrets while you can, Sandy, so you'll not wish you had later. There really ARE 'Secrets' as you've learned.

"Yes, I have a copy of the letter to you. Something told me to write and keep it. I'm so glad I did. A version of it will be in the book underway — but with no way to disclose any of confidences nor embarrass anyone.

"Should you wish to write the lady in New Zealand who has no idea at all who or what I am, nor the Gift of the Child, I give you her address. You know what she might never know — she cannot intimidate you but she will try. Please give her name and address to no one else.

"Yes, I love you Sandy. You must make certain your family understands this Love. I am no threat to your marriage nor your relations with anyone anywhere. YOU know that. So must they.

"I trust you in whatever degree you trust the Child of yourself. 'William Samuel' is in your hands to help or to hurt. The Child of Me is the Child you are too. One Child — made in the Image of God.

"Hang in there! And be patient.

"Love, Bill"

Four

❦

Come to Think of It

I have no idea what "enlightenment" is. All I know is that one day I found myself feeling whole, totally alive and wonderful. And I have not been the same since. The Joy is immutable and simply abides in a sweet sense of peace. I am no longer seeking, just Loving It all for the Unfolding Magic It is. I discovered the powerlessness of the things that happen in this world. I was shown the powerlessness of death and all fear vanished. Yes, the Wonders never cease. I'm rejoicing that whatever this is, it bloomed here in my Heart and Soul. I don't know, I just don't know what it is – but I am most grateful it found me. Simply extraordinary the freedom it brings. I don't know what this is, but I'll take it.

Attachment

I have heard that the Buddha says the root of all suffering is attachment. I don't think that is true. Or his words have been misunderstood. I mean, is he saying we are to avoid attachment? I don't think so. He can't really have been implying that.

We are attached to everything. There is no way we could ever not be attached. Attachment is Love. Love is Life.

Let me suffer. Suffering, feeling like I lost something or someone, leads me to see I am forever attached. Attachment is the holy gift. It is Life. Synergy, together, mixing, connected, combining with and creating something new, bringing about the wholeness from what seems to be parts. I am never separate or apart from Life, nor am I ever separate from the ones I love.

I am attached. Life and I, we are attachment.

If loving another causes me to suffer, then let me suffer. Let life rip me wide open and tear me to shreds and let my heart be broken and let me feel it all. It is the passion of love and the surge of life that fills my being and brings me my salvation, wholeness and peace. I give my heart to break. I give my soul to you – here take it. Take it all.

My feeling of attachment is love and love is the most wonderful thing about life – and the pain of having to let go has been my greatest teacher. It was the agony and pain of loss that showed me Reality. When my heart was torn open Love came rushing in. There in my open heart I saw it so clearly that nothing, no one, no soul, no heart, no loved one is ever lost or unattached.

I am one big living attachment of inseparable togetherness, entwined with Life.

Always and forever here, life never dies. Life is all attached. Each string woven to make the whole thing, this is Life. Life, like a huge infinite tapestry, all the threads are woven together to create the images, the scene, the beauty we see. Life cannot let go of any part of Itself. Nothing dies, no one leaves us, because nothing can ever be detached from Life. It's all here in my heart, within me, so close – in fact, it is all me.

I know I am attached. I exist because I am attached. I am the one living in the completeness of Life. Life is Love, and Love is not going to leave me. I am Love.

I can't lose anyone or anything. I have it all. Even despite the events and happenings that might seem to separate, I am still and always this Love – always.

I love you, my love, always here for you –

Wherever I Go

Wherever I go, there I am. I am here wherever I go. How wonderful that is. What kind of magic trick this life is!

It is both incredible and simple. The Truth is simple, sensational and perfect.

Well, yes, it just looks me in the face with its alluring radiant twinkle and I am blown away. I am just enchanted at how Life is so magical. How is it able to do that trick? I find it amazing. I mean, so amazing to see that Life exists and no one knows how or why, or what it is. This magic is that I am here. Sometimes I can hardly breathe when It suddenly grabs me and takes me like that.

I'm in awe of this whole experience of the unrelenting flawless perfection of the impossible. It's Love.

How can I be *here* no matter where I go? That's It, that's the whole magical, infinite thing of it. It's always here and so am I. We must be attached by some invisible thread. How else does It do this trick? It's got something up Its sleeve. Oh how I Love Its sly hand and secret ways. Life is Magic. God the Magician.

I am just simply enamored and fascinated by Life. I am in love, taken up, swept away in wonder by this strange occurrence of existence.

I'm one big, "Wow man! How'd you do that!?" Astounding – just astounding. The magic keeps pouring in.

And then on top of all this miraculous mystery and magic, we get this additional whipped cream deliciously piled on top of the whole, incredible, tasty delight. We get to experience all this. My god, my dear god, I am so in love, I am bewitched, beguiled by how exquisite Life is.

I will make love to Life, let Life take me like a lover. I and my universe entire are hitched, entwined, intimate, in accord, wed and very much in Love.

I can do nothing but just let it take me, move me, fill me, take all of me, take me. Take me into your arms sweet world, I am yours. It feels so good, so powerful and marvelous – it feels divine.

I love you always and you know –

Snow Days

In Aspen it would often snow at night. Softly falling, light, fluffy snow would cover the landscape. And in the mornings, the sun would break through as the snow storm would pass. I could feel a profound silence when it snowed like that. The snowy stillness felt insulating and quiet. The morning sky would clear revealing the rich color of deep blue velvet. The beauty of infinity was above me, as the big clouds of the storm moved past. Looking up into the sky I could feel the heavenly peace of God as I watched the clouds floating away into oblivion.

On snowy days I would get up early hoping to get a few runs down the hill in the fresh, untracked powder.

Skiing in powder was pure elation. There was an unbound joy of dancing, bouncing, floating, flying through the steep snow-covered terrain.

In order to ski powder I had to let go and let it take me. I could do that, I liked that.

I was not an aggressive skier, so the powder snow suited my ability to dance on my skis rather lightly and yet with an agile strength. I liked wide smooth turns, but I could take a narrow line down the hill if I needed to.

The soft deep snowy powder and I were attuned to each other. We moved together like lovers who feel the union of their bodies and souls. We could feel one another. It was a pleasure to ski with this bounty of beauty that took me.

Weightless on the fresh powder, I moved lively, fast, calm, flexible and dynamic. I can remember well the sparkling glitter of that pristine snow I danced through as it sprayed up and flew into the air. The glittering snow was spinning, twinkling like shredded diamonds as it blew through the crisp, bright winter day. I was in this deep silence there in the forest glens. Riding my skis through the snow was intoxicating. I could feel the holy quiet of the woods. In the silence came ecstasy as I let myself fly down the steep mountain beauty, through the powdery delight.

I was alone in the quiet, at the top of a run, enchanted in a mystical forest. I was wrapped in a soft, silent wonderland of magic and dreams.

Now I see how living my life every day can feel the same way. I am held by Life and I am free, strong, flexible in this interface with Life. I enjoy the adventure of my very own existence. After all there is only Life and I am loving my world. Life is one sacred miracle of love and wonder.

Thank God

Thank God. Yes, exactly, yes the world is perfect because it isn't perfect. The world is perfectly imperfect and that is just perfect, just as it is.

It's certainly true for me. My quest for understanding brought me full circle back to living in the world again, loving all its beautiful imperfections.

Well, not that I could ever really leave Life. But now I know that. I love it for its wild, untamable ways.

Now I see the path to find God or enlightenment was really the desire to escape Life, the thinking that I had to live up to some kind of perfection. Now I know that idea would be the death of me if it were even possible to be perfect. How very sad that is. What I love about me now is how very imperfect I am. That's where the real beauty is.

It turns out Life is perfect because God could not be all that is and leave out imperfection. They say God is Love. Love is then the entirety, all of Life. It includes both *What Is* and *What Is Not* – making it Absolute and Total. Nothing outside of *This.*

Though I didn't know it, I was with the One I Love the whole time. I never went anywhere really. I never left. And Life, Love, God never left me.

Here I am, once again, like a child, floating on that little raft, playing in the bay, laughing, telling stories, enjoying a summer day with my friends.

Yes, I am completely in love and not having to define any-thing, good or bad, perfect or imperfect, as it is simply, totally perfect that it is imperfect. Freedom.

Now, it is my pleasure being alive and full of myself. And, yes, full of my Self. My *Self,* I see, turns out to be the whole wild, untamed Universe. I am the Living Truth I was looking for and I was right here the whole time. It was always here and always me.

So, go ahead, suffer if you suffer, suffer, go for it. Let it hurt. Let Life break your heart, so you are exposed and vulnerable and alive! What the heck? You can't avoid anything. You can't avoid Life. The hard parts about life are the very things that wake us up. If things were perfect they wouldn't be perfect. Indeed, it is the very imperfection that makes it so perfect. The very beautiful imperfections are the things that show us the way Home, back to our Self. If it was not for the "bad stuff" I'd never know the Beauty of Life at all.

You see it is impossible to escape the hard teachings of Life and thank God for that. God really is Love.

Now, I am touching Love, touching this wonder of living. I am Living this wondrous adventure of Something Extraordinary.

Feel it all, feel it all. Love – love, love, embrace and love some more. I'll let it hurt if it hurts – so what, at least I am not afraid, at least I am not trying to avoid anything.

I am the very existence I am. I want to know this Life that is being me being here.

Do what you do and embrace yourself. You and life cannot be pulled apart. So feel it. Just leap in and live. Take a chance, see what happens, find out for yourself who you are. I see how sweet Life is. Life is the very essence of me living. It is my endless being. I am alive, ongoing and everlasting.

And the amazing thing is I don't have to go anywhere to live It. It's all right here where I am. Amazing magic Life is. All right here where I am. I can find the Light of Truth anywhere, because I am It. The marvel of this Presence is always here. One could not ask for more than this.

The future is unwritten, I don't know where I am going. I don't know what will happen. I am on an adventure. I am living chapters in a story wherein I do not know the outcome, or if there even is one. I do, however, have a sense of the plot. It is a love story with a bit of adventure added as zest and spice, and some fast turns on blind, narrow roads that make the story tasty and unpredictable. I don't know how the story ends. The road is uncharted from where I stand, but I know how to keep my heart and soul open. I know how to navigate this wild ride with some balance and mostly with Love leading me. I know how to let go, living fearless and free with this unknown destiny. That I know.

Falling in Love

I always find myself in sweet places with just the right people for the situations. I have been taken good care of by Life. That care often shows up as synchronicity, a magical serendipity.

I met him when I worked at the Country Store. The store had a rustic feeling. The owner designed it to look like an East Coast old-time mercantile. The wooden floors were authentic and she sold penny candy from big jars to add to the country store ambience. Everyone in town shopped there. I knew all my regular customers. And the visitors who came to town, summer or winter, were always fun and happy, delighted to be in such a charming atmosphere. It was a great place to work.

He came in one day to buy some new ski gloves. I remember it well. I showed him several styles of gloves. He tried them on. He was very particular. Or perhaps he wanted to stay awhile and that was his excuse. Who knows, but the sparks were going off like fireworks between us. So his new ski gloves had to be just the right ones. It took some time. But, yes we found them. He was happy. I was happy. We laughed. We flirted. I think we fell in love.

As time passed, we would run into each other on occasion and those short moments of greeting each other were always full of those initial fireworks and sparks. He was irresistible, but I did resist.

One day, perhaps three years down the road from our first encounter, he walked into the little fabric store that I was now managing. That day providence kicked in full force.

I had just given notice to the owner of the shop that I would be leaving in two weeks. I told her I would be heading back to California. It was time for a new direction.

She was on her way to lunch at Toros. While there, she so happened to tell this man who had captivated me the first time I sold him those gloves, that I would be leaving my position at her shop and going back to California.

No sooner had he heard this, he was at the door of the little fabric shop. From the doorway he held out to me an offering of hot enchiladas to-go, wrapped in sparkling tinfoil.

I can't ever forget that moment. He walked in and the smile on his face was absolute shining joy.

There we were, both of us dazzled by each other. He and I, we had this connection ever since we'd first met. Now, when he walked in the door, we were ignited instantly. I always felt something deep in my heart and soul for this beautiful man. That chemistry was there, we connected. We were allured by each other. He was good looking and charming, no doubt about that. There was certainly a powerful physical attraction. But there was more. There was a soul attraction that moved us both toward one another. Not only this feeling of electricity between us, but also something so very familiar and comfortable was there too, as if we'd been in love and adoring each other for forever. He invited pleasure and happiness whenever we ran into each other. I, however, kept my distance as I was staying loyal to another. But now since that other I'd been true to was no longer with me, the doors to a new adventure were opened.

Life is good to me. These things happen. As I have always believed Love is the foundation of everything. Love moves from one lifetime to another, Love goes with us. Life and our relationships here in this time move as one. We know things in our heart. We can trust them. We are Life Itself, Love Itself, not possessors of Life nor possessors of Love. Sweet Life, sweet Love. Freedom.

So there he was standing in the doorway and I felt a powerful sense of serendipity. Blessed wonders. My good luck. My angels at work here. My fortunate planet Jupiter doing its thing. My stars activated, aligned right, shining bright for me. Who knows, but there he was, that beautiful man I'd always loved.

I had not been looking for what was to take place next, but the surprise and unfolding beauty of it all was divine destiny, holy intervention, written before time, perfection.

He smiled, glowing softly and adoringly at me. My joy at seeing him was impossible to contain. My heart just simply knew *this was it*. My smile and the rush of warmth could not be hidden. Something marvelous had just happened. I felt my whole being bursting with passion and joy at the sight of him. I suspect, he could have had me right then and there, at that very moment, taken me among the bolts of fabric.

Yes, right then and there, in that instant, my heart knew I was not going anywhere, my plans had just changed entirely and everything would be alright.

And it was.

Six months later we were wed in the yard of the old stone church in town on a bright and beautiful October day. His two dogs were the only guests.

More Soon

The evening light outside was glowing its halo through the beveled glass windows. I closed the arched, antique-glass doors as I came back inside to sit by the fire. I was still immersed in reading those letters from William. They were powerful and every time I went back over them I gleaned additional insights and wisdom.

"August 6, 1985
"Dear Sandy,
"IT IS IMPORTANT that you and I get together somewhere before I'm gone – important for YOU and the world. Pilgrimages are a necessary part of ones unfoldment and Self-discovery. Most of us go to a hundred places before we've found the RIGHT place and the honest person to visit. You've found Yourself in Me – and I will be able to help you for the troubled times – even as you will help me.

"Yes, it is a trip one must take ALONE in the world for a time. Then we find the Child within. And, if we're supposed to, we find confirmation of the Child 'without,' in the world. Let the Child of you tell you about me. Do you remember the day I asked about the dying trees – and you knew the answer?

"Bring your husband with you, if you like. You'll stay at Woodsong, nestled among the trees, cool and comfortable – everything there that you'll need, the whole cottage to yourself. There are places to walk, drive and do whatever you like. Rachel and I will be next door just a hundred feet up the hill. You will have my little Datsun when you want to explore Alabama. You're welcome as the sunshine – to stay for a week if you want. You may wish to buy groceries, but you'll have no expenses here. The air fares seem to be much less if you agree to a week. There is a

People's Express that flys into B'ham airport, only 45 minutes from here. October is great in Alabama.

"We love you Child of Seven Days. More to you soon. Write when you can.

"On the hill, Bill"

Enchanted Cottage

The beautiful man I married was the man of my sweetest dreams. I felt as if the angels had sent him to me. I knew he was made for me. He had an unconventional sort of rebel nature. He was my lighthouse, always steady and there for me. He knew his own heart and trusted himself. I liked that. We thought alike, we were in agreement.

As soon as we were married we decided it would be a good idea to buy a house and create a home together. After many long weeks of searching all the lovely houses for sale, we found a very special little place. It was an old one-room schoolhouse on Owl Creek Road. We bought it and we were in heaven.

Just like in the fairytales. An old 1930's clapboard school-house with wooden pine floors. It came with a big old-fashioned pot-belly stove covered in shiny nickel embellishments. It was the original stove that used to keep the school children warm many years prior. The place had not been occupied as a school since the early 1950's. Yet, we could still feel the spirit of joyful children sparkling in the soul of that charming one-room schoolhouse. It was well-worn and enchanting. We were eager to expand and create additions to the classic simple style. We both loved architecture, design, building, fine craftsmanship, beauty and creating. We had the same artistic sensibilities and preferences. We both needed harmony and peace in our lives.

We wanted to enjoy our love here and raise a family in this divine home sitting on that perfect piece of land. It was heaven working together.

I knew that our marriage and my life with this man was a treasure. I wanted to care for him and all this good fortune that life had brought to me.

It was a beautiful marriage. He was a good man, devoted, kind and loyal. And if my dear husband, man of dreams, was not holding my hand, he was holding our children, watching over them, keeping them near. He was, for all of us, a strong, loving assurance. He was never overprotective nor possessive in his love. He had this way of calm and balance in all he did. I loved that he was not afraid of things in life, and so the kids also soaked in the benefits of his allowing them to join his adventuresome escapades. He'd take the kids skiing and snowboarding, even on a school day if the powder snow was perfect. He loved to be with our kids and me. He'd taught them to use his carpentry tools, how to climb ladders and build things. And cooking, he adored cooking for its spontaneity, skill and expression of his love, letting the children help him make the pancakes, mixing, adding and pouring them on the hot griddle. Besides such things as showing them how to drive the old Toyota with the stick shift and lessons in hang gliding when they were a little older. He was always at peace, patient, and that reflected in everything he did.

How magical he lived his life. How very loving he was in all ways, always with integrity and honesty, soft and thoughtful of others. He loved beauty, was an artist and a rebel. I appreciated his love for elegance and harmony, music and good food, fine wine, romance, love and laughter.

He listened to me when I'd talk, enraptured by my rambling conversation. He loved my circuitous philosophical revelations, always adoring me as if I was so bright. I loved being loved by him. Everyone always said he lived a kind of Zen-ness in a very natural and innate way. His inner spirit of warmth and light shone so golden, everyone loved that man.

In his soul he seemed to live somewhere outside of the realms of this world, outside the restrictions of matter. There was something ethereal about him. He seemed to move beyond time and space, while yet, still here, able to love all things in this material world of form and beauty. He had something heavenly and mystical about him. He certainly had an authentic charisma. I knew it and I respected those unusual qualities.

We made everything magic. I thrived on the mysteries of life, seeing everything unfold from the mystical perspective. We lived with intentions to make life as good as we could. We lived in a sweet bliss there in our enchanted cottage on Owl Creek Road.

The little schoolhouse grew larger. We designed and added on, we created together. We were expanding our Love, working together, having children together, building more rooms as the family grew.

The kitchen and family room opened up to each other. The big Wolf range, shiny black with six burners, a large griddle and oven was always in use. I loved my stove. It was gorgeous. I loved my home, my husband, my kids and my town.

Our little children were always bubbling with joy and love. Our world exuded happiness and beauty. Life was perfection.

Yes, we lived in a fairytale and that was just how I wanted it.

Our life together was exciting and fun. Nothing I could have ever dreamed would have or could have been so sweet. I was grateful, always grateful. I am fully aware of the good things that lead me.

Owl Creek Road

Our charming home sat at the edge of a small winding creek, surrounded by the natural countryside. The one neighbor was about a half mile away. The solitude and quiet of that creekside cottage was a peace and gentleness that seemed we could touch.

The dirt drive up to the house, the cottonwood trees, wild orchids and iris along the road, the little pond in the summer, the hillside covered in purple sage, all added to that wonderland of love. Groves of aspen trees across the icy creek were gathered in a great wild bunch in the meadow behind the workshop and shed. In the summer the kids would cross the creek, walking over the wood planked bridge they had built. They would play in the aspen meadow among the daisies, having picnics and making boats with twigs and grass to send off down the brook.

Aspen was pure beauty. The town was a delight and full of romance. Nature was everywhere. Each season was a glorious display of divine unfolding abundance.

Summertime was perfect. Flower pots and hanging baskets were filled with red geraniums spilling over in abundance. I loved to decorate the porch with flowers, happy colorful pansies, bright purple and blue lobelia, sweet pink impatiens. Our yard turned into a green lawn of rolling hillside. The grass and aspen trees covered the yard that was dotted with yellow daffodils and periwinkle lilac bushes on the borders. There were raspberry bushes too, filled with a profusion of tasty red berries. It was heaven on earth.

Everything was cared for and loved.

When fall arrived the cords of chopped wood were delivered. The propane tank was filled. Anything that needed repair was done. The easy way of my husband's calm and yet competent and intelligent ability to do so much for all of us kept me from realizing how much he did and how much there was to be done.

He took care of everything, but I was unaware of that. I just knew things certainly ran smoothly around there.

And in the winter, like a little boy, in his well taken care of vintage '58 Toyota, with the snowplow hitched, he would delight in pushing the snow around and keeping the driveway clear. He had a passion for old cars and driving and finding the flow of the Tao with the machinery. He could even turn that cumbersome plow into a supple tool he would use with finesse and artistry.

Beauty is not just an objective thing. I know beauty comes from one's heart, how we live our lives and how we love each other and our world.

Beauty comes to be seen in the essence of the one who is living the Beauty of his soul. We create tangible beauty because we are that beauty on the inside.

The love we felt for each other and our children moved through everything we did.

It goes both ways. Needing to see beauty in my world, in my surroundings in order to feel the beauty in my heart, I create with harmony and love in mind. The beauty in my life around me brings a deeper beauty and peace to my soul. It is my love that makes things beautiful. It is his love that keeps me warm and safe. It is his love that makes my life easy and that makes it easy to give my love, to create with him this sweet paradise.

The essence of everything is holy and sacred. I know this. I can't just learn a philosophy and just speak a philosophy of Life. I know I am required to *live* my philosophy and so I do, I bring love to everything, or certainly being aware of how important this is, I do my best.

Eventually, I came to live this love very open, raw, loose, un-tethered and unpossessed as the totality of my Self. Eventually, I found the fearless love that soars and sails this world in the infinite light, unbridled, unconfined, a sweet and joyful everlasting love, unowned and unleashed.

Line Upon Line

"Sandy, you are among the ones who are capable of the Synergistic Experience – the quantum 'knowing' that allows you to impart your own insights beyond INTELLECTUALISM. Your role in the days ahead hasn't been given to you yet but you will know when your time has come just as I know 'my time' has come to write this to you.

"Love from the hills of Alabama, Billy"

Even when I didn't know where I was *actually* going in my spiritual search, I was still going in the right direction. And when I thought I was going in the right direction, I really wasn't. But it didn't matter, all directions led to the right place – back to me, back to my Self. I didn't know any of that then. I can see it now.

Now I know it would be impossible for anyone to go in a wrong direction.

I see now that this is because there really is no direction. I was always here. *All* is all I am. All paths lead me back to me. It's almost as simple as realizing *I'm always here. I can't go anywhere without me.* I'm It.

Well, that's how it happened for me. But the dawning of this joyful freedom was imperceptible in its slow revelation.

The way to the real, lasting joy and true love was opening up in me. But I didn't see it happening so clearly. I thought I was seeking something out there, something beyond me. I thought I was going to find God. However my search for God led me to my Self. It led me back to me. How beautiful it all turns out to be.

Although, I did have one thing right. I believed, at the time, that this innate sense of Love was the way and was the answer to everything. And I was quite right about that.

I was pretty sure God is Love. I was pretty sure the Truth, Reality, was that *God is the totality of life Itself.* We are living a kind of divine solipsism, I just needed to prove it to myself. Love was a major factor in all this. My heart was always a loving heart, my soul always desiring to love the best I could.

How exactly all my thoughts and ideas about Life would or could all fall into understanding all this and living it, that I was not so sure of.

I had so much, and I trusted Life. I felt God was the answer. I had faith.

No matter what, I wanted to do it my way. I didn't want to find a religion, or a guru or a teaching. I had no inclination to join any groups, communes or cults. I wanted to know God for myself without an intermediary between us. I wanted to know the Truth, Reality, directly.

I knew many things about me. Mostly what I was not – I was not interested in psychology, not interested in religions, Eastern or Western, yoga or meditation. I liked the mystical things, the metaphysical ideas, esoteric ideas, the deeply intuitive things. I did not like rules, restrictions, disciplines, dogma or doctrines.

My rebel soul and iconoclastic nature never wanted to abide within the lines. I wanted to live in the freedom to do this my way. I was willing to find the Truth all by myself, alone. And I wanted to know the Truth no matter what it might be. Even if it meant the very death of me in some existential way. Which, in some teachings, they claim must happen. I was willing, if that be the case.

Eventually the Truth found me precept upon precept. The realizations unfolded inside me. Understanding came to me as I came toward It. Despite my seeking unknowingly in the wrong direction sometimes, this Light still came rushing to find me and It did find me. It was me.

Glorious of all, it ends up the Truth loved me just as I am. Truth was not asking me to get rid of any part of myself, not my ego, not my thinking, not my heart.

It also turned out that what I was looking for was not out there, but here as myself. It was *me*. I was It all along – It was my Self I was looking for.

And this unbound Truth is more wonderful than anything I ever thought it could or would be. It continues, showing me all my ongoing wonder and beauty. I grow richer every day. My spirit, my heart, my soul grows younger. I feel the living vitality of life roaring through me now. I'm the one. It's me.

Silvery Moon

Hey sugar, take your time, enjoy this very dreamy full moon. Tides pull the mind in a languid rhythmic ebb and flow. Easy when you let it take you and you don't mind where you go. Sweet Life. Nothing else like it.

Yeah, I did some research. I enjoy astrology. But I don't know much about it. I sense that those two lovers might get lost in the depths of each other's minds they find so sensual. Such pleasures here under this sort of divinely drunken full moon.

These iridescent-blue moon beams I see are leading me into some strange tunnel of love where this little boat carries me along, as illusions appear to dance in gossamer, twirling gowns, along the river banks. The dense fog is creating misty, watery nymphs, strumming songs that enchant and beguile my vision. I'm swept away in my imagination–or your imagination. Oh my, whosoever it is, it is delectable.

When you speak I see the hot vapors of your mind drifting in lush visions of beauty as your sweet breath forms strange, lovely, delicate, wispy, incomprehensible words in the air. They vanish quickly into the ethers and we laugh.

My heart is always true. I give what I know. What do I know about the cosmic realms? Well, only what I've seen. I get carried away on celestial light and its heavenly music. I'm one besotted beauty, captured by some powerful force of wonder and bliss all day, here in my ivory tower, nestled upon the emerald gardens of God's sweet paradise.

Wonders Beyond Wonders

The sun was going down. It was getting cold out. Inside my little abode, I smiled at the beauty around me. The pine floors gleamed in the light of the evening sunset caught by the beveled glass windows that beamed prismed rays across the room. I put another log in the Vermont Stove. The fire crackled and blazed warmth. I made myself a cup of espresso. My home in the Rocky Mountains was lush with peace and harmony. I adored soaking in the splendor. I was living in heaven right there on earth.

I sat down to read another letter. I felt William knew something about my life that I didn't see yet. I trusted his insights and I trusted his faith in me. I couldn't stop my search anyway, it was my very nature to seek the spiritual things. It seemed to me knowing the Truth was the only way to find authentic under-standing and freedom, if that was ever possible. It seemed to me it was possible. I really had no choice in how compelled I was toward this Light of Understanding that called to me.

What I hadn't expected was how Real this Child is and the genuine inner excitement she evokes. Just as William said, there is this tender and delicious stirring that moves through me now. It is sensual, but it is pristine and innocent. Who will understand this immaculate wonder that I feel? What a surprise to find this tender, delightful Child of myself. This is Real. This peace and aliveness is powerful. I have become my own authority, with a mind of my own. I know who I am. The peace and joy of this Child I am is transcendent, incomparable and inimitable. She is me, she is innocent, pure and perfect. I cannot hold her back.

"May 19, 1984

"Dear lovely Sandy,

"Yes there are wonders beyond wonders – so much more than religionists and metaphysicians suspect. I can and will show you what has been shown to Me. It takes time, as you know, but time isn't what it seems to be and we can talk of THAT.

"Be patient with yourself, Sandy. You will find yourself ever more the Child and ever less the one searching for the Child. You will know you are *her* each time *you come alive with with that especial, tender and delicious Stirring.* Don't begin to think there is anything 'evil' or 'forbidden' about that inner Excitement, Sandy. Just don't talk about it to anyone, yet. The old nature of ourself wants to condemn everything or make us feel guilty. It is better we share that – you and me, alone – until there are others with whom we may share it too. It is a delight, a 'Peace,' the world doesn't comprehend at all – calling whatever we might say of it 'sensual, sexual,' etc. One day, we can talk about THAT.

"I'm sending you more very private pages from my journal. They are for you alone, my Sandy. They relate to your experience (which is my experience) of emptiness wherein you had a Glimpse.

"I love you very much. lady-Child of new light and love, and I hold You close.

"With Love, Bill

"P.S. There is a letter here from your mother which I'll answer soon. I didn't send either letter to Helen. I sent nothing. I haven't forsaken Helen. One day she will find a small measure of

You and your wisdom if she's fortunate. I still see the Child in New Zealand, but I remind myself of the joke about the little boy who was digging through a great mountain of horse manure. 'With all this shit, I figure there's gotta be a pony in here somewhere.'

"Please write, Sandy. I need those feelings your letters communicate of You, as surely as you want them too. Compre? (One day we may talk about THAT. But only face to face – as you learn the mysteries – and if you get here before I'm gone.)

"Don't worry about your words or how you write, just WRITE. The world is waiting for You."

Something Like This

Knowing that I know is the third place. This third place, when we rediscover the Child, this is to enter the kingdom, to live in the meadow, to recognize the sweet wonder of it all. Really, to stake our claim. To proclaim our Divine Inheritance. To pick up our scepter and Live as the Light we really are.

The third place is the Child again, back where I started, but this time knowing what I have found, fully aware and recognizing what a gift this is. This is not going backward, this is going forward to the same place I began, a return. But *new* because there is this added dimension of being able to compare and know This Is It. Now from a higher point of view I take my place *knowing* I know. And more, knowing how very wonderful, liberating and fearless this state of childlike awareness is makes it a whole new world and a fresh, joyful way of life.

I realize the very life of me is a poet, an artist and a mystic. I am a lover of wisdom, truth, freedom, beauty and unbridled joy. Living from this third perspective, this all-inclusive view, I have become my own authority. This is the place of our ultimate, authentic freedom.

Now I see that the whole journey out into the wilderness, into the adult-mistaken mind, getting lost, and hence, making the return trip, was, every bit, absolutely necessary. Every step of the way was all a part of the completeness, the wholeness of this wondrous beauty of Life, this Child's Light I am now living once again.

Finding the third place, returning to the Child, I see this as the completion of the Holy Trinity. The third time's a charm. It takes all three experiences, immersed in an alchemy of Love, in order to find our wholeness and live this Holy Spirit here in the tangible time-space world.

This is beyond wonderful. This is Love! I could not have even wished for something as beautiful and tender and bright. This is extraordinary freedom and all I could ever dream to be.

And yes, I do know.

The Gospel of Thomas (Saying 18) "The disciples said to Jesus, 'Tell us how our end will come to pass.' Jesus said, 'Then have you found the beginning, so that you are seeking the end? For the end will be where the beginning is. Blessed is the person who stands in the beginning. That person will be acquainted with the end and will not taste death.' "

I Love you Angel –

It's Natural

Little children love God. Little children know God exists. They have just come into this world-of-time from the heavenly realms of the timeless. The pristine child-heart still remembers the sublime tranquility and all-encompassing Love. There is no separation between children and this *living illimitable Light* of this heavenly-awareness that they are. They are the pure aware-ness of God's Love. There is no question whether God exists to the child. There is no doubt in this child's heart.

Now, these years later, I can remember again where I have come from and I know the things of my heart. The Child is real. The Child is here with me and I feel this living Presence of God as Life Itself. I am touching God all the time now, because God is this living Self-awareness I am. God is Life. I feel everything. I am alive. I am real.

And it was love that showed me the way back to this holy light that touches me. It was love that brought me Home.

This credulous childlike heart of mine is steady, noble, strong, intelligent, balanced, vulnerable, tender, kind, open, funny, untamed, honest, genuine and real. This living awareness has become me.

It was this divine guidance, this inner directing call that has always been here with me. This has always been who I am and includes who you are.

This holy Child sits next to Reality and Is forever touching me and holding my heart. It is my guide and my soul. It is my mind and my body here in time. Nothing is outside of this light of awareness, this living identity I am.

Philo Sofia

Is it my Sagittarius sun or is it in my Scots-English rebel genes? Or just the way Life is? I am a lover of freedom and I am a natural born philosopher. I can't help it. I was born with the spirit of the true *philo sofia*. My mind goes toward the higher visions very naturally. I see the bigger picture. This heart of mine perceives with the distant longings, and moves toward the spiritual call. I wanted to know what was behind it all. I wanted to understand what Life was about, I wanted to know God. I could understand the wild passions of Don Quixote. He lived in my soul too. My questing nature was inherent, my philosophical way of seeing Life, my perceptions, my poetic, artistic soul, and the rebel, I see now, are inherent.

My good fortunes started at a very young age. As a baby child, my parents took me and my siblings to many of the lavish parties hosted by my godfather who was part of the Hollywood film industry.

We would drive from our beach home into the summer heat of the foothills of Los Angeles, the San Fernando Valley, to join the fun.

As a child, I enjoyed observing the people at those parties. There was a lot of drinking, laughter, teasing and playing. Amidst it all were the steaks sizzling on the big outdoor, brick grills. The aroma of the grills mixed with the laughter and warm sun was exhilarating. I was captivated by my senses as a child. The sights and sounds return to me easily now. I recall the picnic tables set with red and white checked cloth and a full spread of food for everyone. There was a bounty of colorful bowls of fruit salad, potato salad, cakes, cookies, hamburgers and steaks and plenty of drinks everywhere. Joy and delight filled the air.

I would wander off alone. I would watch the stylish men and women on the tennis courts. I would stroll down the long driveway by myself. I could feel everything. The impressions were palpable. The wet floor of the dressing rooms by the pool. The sultry air mixed with the smell of chlorine. The joyful screams of kids splashing and playing in the water. I loved the hot air and the waves of fragrance moving off the eucalyptus and pepper trees. I would feel and hear the crunch of the earth as I'd walk over to the clubhouse. The clubhouse was a large old home on the estate. I'd go in through the back kitchen door where the cooks were working and go into the library.

The rooms were dark, cool and elegant. My bare feet felt the soft rich silk of the Persian carpets. The lamps were aglow in the dim light even during the day. The drapes were always closed. There was no sunlight in there. I played in the library with my friend Sherri. Her father kept his polo ponies at the club. He had a station wagon. It was almost all wood on the outside. I loved riding in that car. The car had a dark burgundy-red hood and a navy blue roof. It smelled like hay and horses. The leather of the bridles and saddles had such a wonderful aroma. All that horse equipment was in the very back of this rather wonderful car. We would all climb in to go see his polo ponies.

Sometimes Sherri and I played in the clubhouse. We would sit crossed legged on the soft silky rug and play checkers and cards, or we'd get a big book of famous old artwork or European architecture down from the shelf. Interested and fascinated we'd create stories about the images. We were surrounded by art and fine crystal vases and exquisitely upholstered chairs. The rooms had an aura of mystery and beauty. All of it was just what I loved.

Eight acres of beauty. The road leading up to the clubhouse went past the little white chapel in which I had been christened. The long drive up to the main house had a white fence perfectly appointed. We drove along under the eucalyptus trees and the pepper trees, the flickering sunlight dappled the way. The dusty air was infused with the fragrance of a hot day. I was filled with the anticipation of fun and good times.

I was delighted by my world.

Remarkable Friends

In Aspen, in our home, I was content and grateful for the perfect life of abundance, love and beauty that seemed to follow me everywhere.

Before we met, my future husband worked at the Crystal Palace in the kitchen. He was a lovely friend to everyone, always respected and liked by those who worked with him. Eventually he bought into his own restaurant with a partner to become the owner of Toros, a very popular restaurant in town.

A few years after we married, we opened another restaurant called Poppies Bistro Cafe. It was considered one of the best in town at the time, a wonderful place with fabulous food and a wine list that would please any sommelier. Notable guests crowded the tables, wealthy politicians, shahs, Arabian princes and oilmen, notorious writers and the wild celebrity crowd of actors and well known singers and rock band idols.

My husband's authentic and gracious style kept the cafe feeling unpretentious, warm, friendly, comfortable and elegant. And his love for beauty was expressed in every detail. Candles glowed soft light against dark red walls creating a sense of privacy, while the small bar area invited happy socializing. The bar of polished cherrywood had been handcrafted by my brothers, both fine woodworkers. Poppies was charming and fun and always packed full during the skiing season.

We had a lot of freedom to do as we wished. Aspen was a seasonal place, so time for travel during the off-season was to our advantage. We took the kids to Hawaii and the Caribbean. We traveled to England, across Europe to Greece. We stayed in a chalet in Chamonix for two months and explored the Amalfi Coast and Provence while there.

But, when Independence Pass was open, one of our favorite little jaunts was to drive up and over the mountains and down the other side into Santa Fe, New Mexico. We had spent our honeymoon in Taos and Santa Fe. We both loved that area. We would head for Santa Fe rather often because the time there was always – well, yes – enchanting.

So, one enchanting day, there in Santa Fe, probably around 1980, I discovered the man who would become my spiritual teacher and guide. There we were in a little bookstore. I was looking through the shelves, lost in the wrong section, when I found just the right book. It was titled *A Guide to Awareness and Tranquillity* by William Samuel.

I bought the book and began to read it. I think I read the whole entire book without putting it down. For me, this was the message I had been looking for. I was reading things in this book that explained to me all that I knew but that I could never quite put together into such perfect words.

I fell in love with Mr. Samuel's work instantly.

Awareness and Tranquillity

From William Samuel's book *A Guide to Awareness and Tranquillity*, I read these words and the feeling in my heart was like hearing a song. And destiny took my hand.

"Awareness itself is our Identity. Awareness is being aware. Awareness is beholding. We are this Awareness aware whether we take thought or not. As Awareness only (not the possessor of it), we simply view things without judgment; without planning and calculating; without comparison and criticism; without dividing and subdividing and without making a critical analysis of everything. As Awareness we behold! We muse wholeheartedly. We enjoy color and form. We examine the infinite detail of

Deity. Effortlessly, we see the precision and perfection of the ALL that NOW is!

"In so acting, I assure you we are not worrying about the blunders of yesterday or of what might happen tomorrow. As Awareness, one is active NOW, and – listen carefully – NOW is all right! NOW is always all right!

"Life is unencumbered NOW. Awareness is free NOW; but the very minute one starts labored thinking, the instant he begins planning, calculating, reasoning, judging, criticizing, condemning and worrying, the NOW seems covered with a veil, and we have plunked ourselves right back into the middle of the cause-effect area of human activity called 'the seeming dream.' The start of that dream is personal thinking, thinking that is not the great necessity the world makes of it. The time for thinkers is coming to an end.

"NOW is now already. It needs nothing to help it along. 'The world is a perfect vessel,' wrote the sage. 'Perfection is spread over the whole face of the land,' says the Christ."

I knew then that this was the teacher for me.

"'HE SHALL RETURN TO THE DAYS OF HIS YOUTH'

"Those who study this 'philosophy' with us on Lollygog are always amazed to find a return of youthfulness, not only in outlook but in action and appearance. Why should there be surprise? To *be* this NOW of UNJUDGING Awareness is to l*et go* the great weight of opinions, notions, prejudices, quirks and idiosyncrasies which, added to personal memory, are all there is to 'age.' It is the one who acts as though he *possesses* life who ages and seems to suffer the decline and death of the deceiver.

" 'Hast thou not known? Hast thou not heard, that the everlasting God (who is Being all there is to the Awareness reading these words) fainteth not, neither is weary? He giveth power to

110

the faint; and to them that have no might he increaseth strength . . . but they that wait upon the Lord [they who will simply *be* the unjudging, motiveless Awareness we be] shall *renew* their strength; they shall mount up with wings as eagles; they shall run and not be weary; and they shall walk and not faint.'

"When one lets go the worried plans intended to improve the already perfect NOW, he discovers the Self that 'turneth the shadow of death into the morning.' 'The former things are passed away . . . and there shall be no more death.'

" 'If there be a messenger . . . an interpreter, one among a thousand, to show unto man his uprightness . . . his flesh shall be fresher than a child's; he shall return to the days of his youth . . . and his life shall see the light!' "

This was a teacher that suited my taste. He was down-to-earth, unpretentious, humorous and brilliant.

And I liked his straight forward ways. He did not want me to stand on my head, or sit cross legged and try to still my mind, or stop thinking. He asked nothing of me really, but to listen to my own heart.

I had found a teacher who believed in freedom and self-governance. William's style gave rise to a genuine peace and passion in me. His work was not related to any organization, which pleased me immeasurably. And I appreciated that this study was not part of any religious group or special theology, not related to one church more than another, or to one metaphysics more than another.

He reiterates often that the Truth is the Truth is the Truth, available to anyone and everyone, no matter our life's situations.

I said, "Yes!"

He said the Truth is not strained through any organization, nor does Truth follow any particular line of teachers. "The Truth includes all that has ever been construed to be any and every teacher, philosophy or holy book."

And I said, "Yes!"

He said "the Truth we are concerned with is the truth of the Single Selfhood being the awareness of these words. There is one Truth only – the fact of Identity – the truth I am."

I said, "Yes!"

I found the teacher who was right for me and my tendencies toward independence, my rebel nature and artistic sensibilities. William was a lover of freedom and the individual's ability and necessity to know first hand, directly, this Living Source, the Wellspring behind all life.

Here, with William Samuel, there was no idol worshiping and no request for a secondhand intervening "guru" to come between me and Reality.

He didn't refer to himself as a teacher because he didn't want to be put on a pedestal or seen as an authority figure. He told us the Truth is within ourself, we are our own teacher and authority, no one else. I had found an honest man in whom I could trust that I might find myself, whatever that might be.

Jesus said: "Blessed are the solitary and elect, for you shall find the Kingdom."

Joy of joy, every word he wrote confirmed my own heart-felt understanding that Life, Identity and God are really one-and-the-same and that I could find and know this Presence directly. He had no restricting disciplines or practices. This would be my own way that leads me to the Truth. It would be my own words that would guide me to find for myself the direct and genuine connection to the Source.

I had already established long ago that God is the Presence, Life, Awareness and Everything that life is. God is Life Itself. From the time I was a little girl, I knew that there was nothing but God and God's Light. As a grown-up, my intellect thought it needed more. I felt something was missing. I also knew that this search would be between me, my heart and God alone.

As soon as I finished the book, I called Mr. Samuel. We spoke for an hour or so and we got along beautifully. We began writing and exchanging letters. A correspondence that lasted many beautiful years.

My meeting with Mr. Samuel was another magnetic, divinely decreed connections in my life. He became my enduring friend and my mentor.

Eventually, as he guided me aright, and with my own honest and sincere heart, I did find peace. I did find my Self again, and my freedom. And I am now immersed in the deep wellspring of this Infinite Presence. I am forever grateful to that man for his honest Light.

This abiding Peace and Love is real. I have been totally transformed by this rediscovery – this I know.

In many spiritual studies there was always talk of childlikeness, the Christ Consciousness, and being children of God, but there was not such a direct and unflinching message about this living expression of the Child as my own unbound awareness, life and soul. But, some years later William presented these ideas in his final book, *The Child Within Us Lives! A Synthesis of Science, Religion and Metaphysics*, wherein he stated clearly, without hesitation, that there was a third step in the journey to wholeness, that our time of understanding is not complete until we find the Child, our original nature, ourself. Thank God for William and his one last book in my life.

William speaks of the Child in terms of an actual reality of myself. He tells me this pristine, pure, immutable Self is myself, right here and now. Not far away nor difficult to be. I am It, now. I am capable of returning to this original state of mind and living it again.

I trusted him. I knew he was a good and honest man. I knew he was among the truly enlightened. He had lived every word he wrote and shared with me. I knew if he told me there was this Child to seek and that I would find It, I could believe him. And so, I would keep my heart open to find and to know It.

Now I know – finding this Self of myself, the heart of myself, the Child of me – this is real, this is the Way.

The Girl From Aspen

"And suddenly you know: It's time to start something new and trust the magic of beginnings." –Meister Eckhart

It was as if we'd been old friends from the start. William was clearly one of those mystical, magnetic encounters in my life.

I recall the first time we actually did meet. My husband and I took our two little girls over to Pueblo, a town where William was giving a talk. We arrived a little late. I sat down quietly in the back of the room. My husband took the kids over to a big county fair going on near by.

William and I had never actually seen each other in person before that night. He had no idea I was there.

William was talking to the group. He asked the crowd of people a metaphysical question. A question about the dying trees. No one raised their hand. He kept looking at the group anticipating someone to answer.

I was not, at that time, anyone who would easily speak up. But something welled up in me. I knew the answer. I had to take a chance and volunteer my thoughts, dare, for better or worse.

I spoke up. William, still not knowing I was the young lady who had been corresponding with him recently, was very happy that I was attempting to answer his question about the trees. My answer seemed to please him. To my joy my answer brought a big smile to his face. His eyes twinkled at me and I was delighted as he said to the small crowd, "Yes, yes, she got it! She said it very well! That's it!"

Then, during the break, while the little gathering of folks went to enjoy some refreshments, William asked me to come sit next to him. I did. I introduced myself. He then realized I was *the girl from Aspen* whom he had been corresponding with.

He seemed to be so pleased with me. I was proud of myself that I had trusted myself and answered his question – and that I had the right answer.

So, we became long time friends. We wrote to each other, visited each other several times, and called each other many times over the years.

William's wife Rachel also became my good friend. She was sweet and kind and always there for me. Rachel was a beautiful lady. She worked hard to keep William safe and comfortable so he could bring his message of Self-discovery to those of us who had this deep desire for an honest, tested and proven understanding and Truth.

Every Bit Is Good

The kids were all home from school now, fed and settled into their homework. The house was quiet and cozy. It was getting late, but I went back to the box of old letters. Taped to the top of this letter was a small red and brown bird feather, a gift from William.

"Woodsong 4-23-89

"Sweet Sandy of My Heart,

"I spend this Sunday morning with you to answer your good and honest letter.

"Listen Lady; you are saying it very well. You are communicating. You are being heard. You are making progress upward — and, it seems to me here in the hills of Alabama, that Sandy is doing marvelously.

"There is a place near the top of DaShan where the five paths merge into one. That single pathway is only one Child wide and one walks it absolutely alone. Or, that's how it seems. Actually, we are surrounded by unseen Angels at that time, in front of us, behind us, on both sides of us. And I am there too, encouraging you, encouraging, unseen.

"This is the final part of the DaShan experience. It can be terrifying. It is straight and narrow. Its final ascent is perfectly even and requires patience, fortitude, discipline and true balance. You will make it Sandy. You will make it in tangible fact because you are already being the Goal in Truth. The human experience follows in Fact, like an echo.

"In the next few echo years in time, I think the world will be shaken mightily — just as the sciences finally reach the Answers about what it is all about. In that regard, enormous things are happening. Sandy, just keep recording and remembering your steps and how you are going from one view to another to another, changing all the time. Soon you emerge at the peak (where you came from and where you are returning) where all the past views appear simultaneously. I had no one to tell me what was happening. You will be able to lead the way for others. Everything Good has conspired for good reasons to lift you where you are.

"Tender Lady, the best is yet to come! And every bit of it is Good going on! For now, just believe that. In humility, just thank God and believe that naught but Good is going on. Hang in with that! Something marvelous is happening for Man and His World.

"I know what leads you Sandy, and I trust you. You are important to us all.

"You are much Loved, Bill"

William had, I do believe, seen my future, but I didn't know that at the time. I understood his words, but considered them only to be metaphor. I was prepared to face an esoteric journey on a path to understanding and enlightenment, but I had no idea how much I would have to sacrifice, tangibly and unwillingly. The paradox is that I would have had to face the sorrows that are unavoidable in life whether I had taken this path or not. But without this Light that leads me, I would not have been able to make that final ascent into this abiding Peace. The final ascent did indeed require my fortitude and discipline, but most of all it required the trust that "naught but Good is going on."

Yes, he had known what was to come and that I would make it through, find my way, and more, be able to show the way to others. I had no idea about any of this, nor that I would, one day, bring my heart to my world, share my road map that might lead others to this treasure, the sweet illimitable love, peace and joy that has found me.

Love, God, Billy and Me

Over the years there was much communication between William and me, phone calls, letters and visits. Bill and his wife Rachel loved to visit us in Aspen, and we enjoyed staying with them at Woodsong in Alabama.

Billy's profound conversations with me were always heart-to-heart. He told me many things that I would listen to and learn from and eventually live.

I was learning. I was growing. I was being transformed, even if at times subtly and unknowingly, by every new glimpse and glimmer of Light. Each insight was moving me along to new higher vistas, yet always including the lesser view.

If we are open and willing, life will be our teacher. And a fine teacher life is.

A main gift and point was that I was to *find the beginning*. Then, from that beginning, *live* everything from the *knowing* of this identity I found there, "not the personal sense of things, not the world's ideas, opinions and judgement of things. We 'begin' with God, the ALL that Isness is, and rejoice at the wonders this ever new view reveals. We LET that Mind be us which IS the awareness of the Truth we are."

If things became distressing or worrisome, I would return to the beginning, to the fact of God's Allness. Standing there in that Light of Truth a sweet relief would wash over me. This was my steady and faithful foundation, which I could immediately return to because it is always here and now.

Billy always pointed me back to Awareness. Awareness, right here, right now, is the common denominator which includes all that is. Awareness is Primary and exists before time-space-matter. Really seeing this, this is my freedom now. This is It, simple and easy and profoundly life changing.

William wrote "Awareness is not separate from the images within It any more than the television screen is separate from the cowboys and commercials there. Therefore, we can see that our identification as awareness ITSELF is not a withdrawal from the world, from people or from the adventure of living. It is a withdrawal from our own valued opinions, notions and prejudices of them." Such a beautiful metaphor.

This I understand now. I know this now. I see the totality of my Self and I Live It. I really can't do otherwise. I know this is all I can live and all that *is* real. This is the happy Child rediscovered, this is all that I am.

This is not a denial of the world. When we come to understand the images then there is a revitalized interest in everything that appears here in this world, "in everything that appears as conscious identity as this Awareness."

I see now, just as he said, yes, It is everything. This Self, this life I am, this identity, this presence I am includes everything. This life I am includes Life entirely, fully, all of it, images and that which is behind the images, all-inclusive Life. Now I live fearlessly.

As I live this childlike-awareness-being, I am effortlessly aware. I find this daily experience expanding into undreamed of new action. And I find I have the strength and means necessary for that action.

I am this sweet boundless Self-awareness. I am the pure state of childlike awareness that sits here right now at the right hand of Reality/God. I am forever and always here as all-inclusive Life. I am the child, the soul, the light and love that God is.

The little girl I was, bold and happy, she has come back to me. She is my one true heart. She is my messiah and redeemer. She lets me understand things that once were nearly impossible to see and know.

If we are sincere in our search, life will not give up on us. Life Itself is the discipline. We cannot escape the hard teachings and we should not want to.

It was the pain and loss and sorrow that led me home. It was the living of the "hard teachings" and embracing them, not trying to escape life. It was using every situation as a lesson that led the way to freedom and the return home.

Now, in freedom, I am not trying to make life secure and safe, or perfect. Now I am free from fear and I am living the sweet totality of life, always in love with it all. The images are harmless and yet this is the joy and wonder of life. All means *all*, and life includes all the images within it, within my Self.

Losing something I most cherished turned out to be the proverbial last straw, the thing that brought me home.

Losing all I had placed so much value in and then realizing where the Real value, where the changeless and eternal Life is, this is the genuine freedom.

Life will do the work for us. Life will uncover and reveal the Truth to us. Sometimes even if we do not want to see it, it will show us anyway. I had no choice but to let It show me the way.

I had to yield to this Ineffable Love, and when I did, it was very good. I had to let Life do what it does. Then, out of the shocking daze, to look up and around and see that everything was returned to me, that all was truly divine and very good. It is Love and it is *all good*. I ended up reaping all that was Real, the Living Holy Spirit, the Unseen Eternal Love and all the benefits of this Love's powerful beauty and intelligence. I found freedom through surrender. I came Home. Now, all I thought I had lost was returned to me and added to, ten times ten, in ways only the Heart can understand.

Five

Unbound Love

Dear love, dear one, sweet angel I love you. I will bring you up high with me. Come sail on wings of Love with me across the infinite sky of wonders and glory.

The whole Truth is about Identity. God and I, you and me and This. God adores me. I include you. You include me. Thee and me and God make three. Well, yes, God adores thee and me. That I know, I have seen the gifts, the confirmation, the proof of this adoration.

Now the marvel continues to grow and speeds forth as this great pleasure in bringing you a love letter. Bringing you my barefoot heart. This is what I am here to do. To bring this love song and sing it so that it touches you and lifts you high.

I am an artist and a poet, so I am here to paint you a picture of love that will move you deeply and bring you back home to your soul, to find your own freedom.

And I am going to give you my heart. I love you. I love the beautiful, unique expression of divine Love you are. You are a conscious treasure, a jewel of distinction. Your fire lit, burns bright. Stand wholly and holy in your Light, the fire of your Soul, the everlasting value of your Reality.

I had no idea this sweet surprise of joy would come along. My sweet heretic, noble and true. This life I live has been a windblown perfection unfolding for me. Wild ride across the Pleiades as I gaze upon the desert sky studded in brilliant stars that shine a path into the beauty of your mind.

The Universe brings us our destiny. It is written before time. We just live with our heart open and keep moving with the flow, living Tao. Like Lao-Tzu whose name means Ancient Child. I am the Child again. The Child is the Master, the Child knows.

No more a slave to fear. No more. Sweet freedom comes as the heart whispers love in lyrics heard as quiet breath all through the night. I feel the power of your music, nourished by love's soft voice. To be noble and royal, reaching the goodness of those heavenly ideals of love and truth and light. Reach. It is here and you can take what is yours.

Dear Life

I would be enfolded in that beautiful home on wintery days, the old stove burning warm, the logs crackling and snapping in flames. I cuddled into my sanctuary, my life, and my love, my sweet Owl Creek home, and I wrote. Writing and reading were my favorite things to do. I could be alone with myself for hours. I have always enjoyed being alone, I have always liked my own company in the quiet.

On summer days, out on the porch, I had the cool mountain breeze and blue sky to keep me company. I spent much of my time soaking up the beauty of my days and the bounty of life that surrounded me. My chores done, I had my pen and paper in hand. I enjoyed writing, thinking, pondering life, contemplating and speculating.

Just give me my hot cappuccino and the silence of my home and I would be completely content. With that, I would be set to write, finding a way to put my own insights and wisdom and glimpses into words. I loved writing in my journals.

As William would tell me, "There could be no words in all the world more important to you than your own." This is true for each of us.

William's suggestion to write as a form of meditation suited me well.

I really loved this practice of "journal tending" – this meditative writing. It was a perfect path to Self-discovery for me.

Very often my meditative journals became letters to William and to my mother. I would send my notes to those two loved ones. I enjoyed trying to express my heart's mysterious visions and flashes of clarity and insight.

They loved receiving them too. William always said I had an ability to write and more, he loved the joy he felt in my words, behind the words. William would write back to me and tell me in his own elated words that I was on my way and that one day I would "teach, and publish and chart the course for others." He saw things about me that I did not see.

Home and Heart

The interior of the home, being an expression of the heart of me, meant that our home would and should exude love and beauty. I believed that the tangible, literal home was the outward reflection of me. In many ways we all walk into the interior of our soul when we walk into our own homes. The two are one. Life always reflects who we are. Homemaking, for me, is making love, showing love, bringing love to those we love. It is an act of love made tangible and visible.

One day, with time on my hands, I decided I just might be able to paint something other than the warm, rich colors I would create for the interior walls of our home. Maybe I could paint in other ways, maybe I was an artist after all.

I signed up for an art class.

I showed up with the required paper, pencils and paints. We were a small group of about eight. The teacher began. It was in a class room much like every other school room. That prison kind of thing. I had the urge to leave. I felt a slight sense of mental suffocation being there. I felt like I was back in time. The teacher seemed to be duplicating the same art class I'd failed in high school. I was expecting something new and creative and interesting to learn, but that was not happening. I was thinking to myself that at least there is a nice breeze blowing through the open window and at least I can enjoy the sounds of the children on the playground outside.

I have always loved the uninhibited laugher and joyful screams of children playing in schoolyards. The children were shouting and having fun. The play yard was down the hill and quite some distance from the room we were in, so the noise had a nice background ambience to it. The sound of kids playing is very soothing to me. The kids outside were not interfering with anything. To me, the fresh breeze and sounds of the children's carefree squeals and shouts were the only thing I was enjoying.

Suddenly one of the women in the group gets up and goes over to the open window, she slams it shut, saying something about how she can't stand the noise from that playground.

After that first day at art class, I never went back.

Liberation

I went home and began to paint without any instructions. Liberation, I would just do whatever came to me to do on that big white canvas. I would experiment. I would trust my heart's vision. I would trust what would appear on that empty paper and let the painting paint itself. I just wanted to play and enjoy those gorgeous colors and brushes and pencil.

Painting is magic. I was enthralled watching what appeared upon that blank paper. I was seduced by the alluring, exquisitely rich paints. I was in wonder and delighted to see how the paints would find their way into expression. I loved to hold the brushes, feel them in my hands, feel their bristles, touching them to know which one I want to use for this or that. I loved the freedom to not care what happens or what turns up. I enjoyed the magic of what appeared out of nothingness.

Something always unfolded before me on my paper and the whole affair was always astounding to me. I was impressed and surprised at what was created from this alchemy of mixing spirit and matter, mixing seen and unseen.

Enjoying the process, I was in a state of serenity, entranced, as I painted. Painting is sensuous, the touching and seeing, even the scents of the paints. I loved the swish of water on the brush. There is this love between me and what comes to be seen. Love making, creating, letting, allowing, open and giving as I paint. I reach into a vision somewhere within me. Then, in pure wonder, it emerges in front of me.

Tubes of colors, luscious colors to squeeze, to see the paints ooze out into this rhapsody of blending and mixing and creating. I am transported to paradise through this alchemy when I paint; my state of mind is in the very beauty I wish to bring forth.

The beauty can't be painted the way it is felt. But it can often be felt permeating the artwork, expressing an essence of my heart somehow into a vision living there upon the paper. I am a bridge into the invisible worlds. A portal standing open, giving and receiving between the intangible and manifest.

When I paint, I am the textures, the brushes, the moving, flowing, strokes of freedom and lines of definition, watching that divine something doing it all on its own. It is my pleasure to be the recipient of this beauty. I am the conduit between imagination, idea, spirit and matter, heart and soul made tangible.

Unleashing the carefree child artist, letting go any fear of criticism, I found this bold and unintimidated spark of myself, the Child. I recognized her. She was someone I had always known. The unlimited soul of me was an artist.

And so I am an artist. I want to share my heart with you. I will give you my heart in my words and in my kisses, in love for you, in my colors, my touch. This is me giving my life to my beloved Life. Loving me loving you is being the warp and weft of all that I am. I am my own sweet pleasure enveloping your beauty and merging with your light and love. That is what life is. It is a feeling of making love. It is the intermingling of ourself with everything. One big love fest, I dare say.

Finding the Child

Morning arrived and my husband made me one of his very special espressos. He whipped the hot milk to a fluffy froth and added it to the rich, thick coffee in my cup. My husband had gone out earlier and gotten some fresh homemade bread too. I made some toast. I had everything I could ever want.

But, within me, something was still not settled. I felt I was here in this world for more, that I was to find the answers to this strange disquiet, this *something* that constantly allured me deep in my soul. I felt I must find it. I was restless. I felt I must follow this desire for a deeper understanding of life and who I am. I sensed I was here for *something,* but I didn't know what. The call was unrelenting.

Outside on the porch again, I pulled another letter from the disorganized bunch. This one was exceptionally moving and passionate. I was enraptured and thrilled with it. This letter had changed me from the first time I read it.

"Dear Sandy,   September, 1992
"Sit easy as you read this.

"Clearly you are a lovely lady. Clean and decent and pure, 'Worthy of my secrets.' I cannot wave a wand and make all pain and anguish go away – but they will go away! Line upon line, precept upon precept, here a little, there a little.

"If anyone has ever attained to the Secret of the Child within without human anguish, I have never seen or heard of him. 'Blessed is the man who has suffered, he has found the life.' Sandy, be assured that your inner turmoil is not in vain; it is not for nothing; it is not anything you are guilty for. Rather, it has been as necessary for you as it was for me – as it is to every small and large creature emerging from its self-spun darkness.

"Here is a mystery:

"The little girl of yourself is still present within you.

"In the world's belief, the child of us gives way to adulthood with all the anguish of growing up, growing older, marriage, family and all the rest of the world's tribulation. But the little girl of you is still very much alive, Sandy.

"I ask you to DO the following which will prove it:

"If you will take a quiet walk this evening, the Child of you will go with you. If you let her, she will see the pathway, the grass, the trees and mountains for you, just as you remember her

127

seeing them when you were an absolutely carefree child. Anticipate that as you go for your walk.

"If you walk quietly tonight, mindful of the Child of yourself,
she will let you hear the distant sounds and smell the evening
fragrances exactly as she let you hear them and enjoy them when
you were that wonderful 7-year-old.

"Gentle Sandy, that little girl you were doesn't feel the
anguish of the world nor anything wayward. The pure, simple,
credulous pristine Child of us doesn't give two hoots about religion or mysticism or human problems. She holds God's hand
eternally, fearlessly, joyfully, calmly, filled with awe and wonder,
excitement and surging love.

"That is the Child I send this letter to. That is the Child I
know you were Originally – and are now. That is the Child YOU
know you are as well. She is the one I saw from the first time I
met you those years ago. She hasn't gone anywhere She hasn't
been destroyed by time, guilt, mistakes, age nor anything else.
The Child of us seems to leave us in human time. It is supposed
to – hidden for a long time in time – thence to be rediscovered
and reborn right out here in time's sequential unfolding. She is
the Original Christ Child of us, closer than fingers and toes,
closer than breathing, waiting to be re-acknowledged, called
forth and rediscovered.

"Walk with her tonight, Sandy. Look at the stars as you did
those years ago. Be still and patient. Something will stir within.
You will feel Something deep within yourself. That greater than
sensual marvel stirring within is the Christ Child of Yourself telling you that you are coming alive again and coming home again;
that your longings can be fulfilled; that you have important
things to do here in this arena of time and space.

"Hear me once again, Sandy with the strawberry hair: Your
own Child Selfhood is still alive! You will be looking at the world
through those True Eyes again. I promise you that because I

128

know what I have found for myself. The Child of you is the Child of me is the Child of Everyman. 'Lest we become as children...' it is said.

"Tonight, in the quiet of your walk, feel that grand Marvel within yourself – nothing less than the kingdom of Heaven itself. That marvel we feel can grow into Something a hundred times more marvelous than anything we have ever imagined before. You and I are holding hands there, Sandy. We are One with God and with all children. We joy uninhibitedly with a holy delight within.

"Religion knows a little about the Child, but has rather misdirected attention to a figure 'out there' in linear history. Metaphysics knows nothing of the Child at all! Isn't that interesting? But, don't misunderstand; metaphysics is subjectively correct. It is a PART of the Mystery. Religion's misdirection is correctly part of the Mystery, too.

"I have more to tell you as you find the Child! Your time will come, lady who laughs and cries and worries about her children. The first Child to concern yourself with is the one within. That one takes care of the others.

"Walk through the Door tonight, Sandy. Walk on beyond your fears. See how very much alive you are still. Something Wonderful will walk with you tonight. Watch and see.

"Love from Woodsong on a misty morning, birds singing extra special for you and me – and everyone.

"I love you, Billy at Woodsong"

I remembered back to the very first time I had read that letter and just how much it had changed me. I recalled that I did do what he asked. I took a walk down our road that very evening. And, it was true, I did walk through a door that night. It was quite remarkable what happened. Yet, it all came to me so subtly and softly and imperceptibly. The Child was found, arriving ever so gently on my walk that night. I could feel a small sense of it, a little glimpse, a stir from deep within. Memories of childhood started to return and I let them come back to me.

I didn't know how deeply I'd been changed, but I know now something extraordinary had happened on that evening walk. I know now the seeds were planted on that night.

It took some time from that moment on, but the seed took root, the sprout began to grow within me and it began to grow up toward the heavenly sky and out toward my beautiful, tangible world again. I was finding the Child.

Now I know. This is more than I could have hoped for or wanted. There would have been no way to this unbound Love except through this childlikeness of my Self rediscovered.

The transcendent Self of you, the Child, is your Soul. It is your own living authority, not beholden to human governments or religions. The Child you are is strong, wise, bold and solitary, no longer slave to dogma or doctrine. This Holy Essence of yourself knows how to navigate this world through dominion, grace, intelligence and the Light of greater understanding.

Years Later

Now that this Child has come fully alive in me, now as I write this book, now I am living this truth I longed for. The Child has come back to me. It is real and it is a joy beyond anything I could have dreamed. Life is an ongoing wonder that proves the Child's spirit is real, proves it to me every day as it flows through me and through my life. I see the evidence, the fruit of Its presence in my life all the time, every moment of my days. It is undeniable. I have been made new, youthful and alive, and returned to the one I have always been.

The joy of being brings its magic with it.

The wildest part is I feel just like I did when I was a little girl. An energy and enthusiasm surges through me, day and night. Sensuous, carefree, unrestricted, I am alive and enjoying the world, like I did as a child, feeling safe and whole again.

I know what this is. This is the mystical experience, the holy union, and it proves itself as I live it. I see its beauty doing for me what it is here to do. It brings me patience and stamina, kindness and generosity of mind and spirit. It brings me the light of knowing right from wrong. I know when I go off course. I know when I stay true to myself and when I am right on target. If I go too far, I readjust easily, swiftly. I know how to return to my beloved equanimity. I am made new, but everything about me remains so familiar and comfortable. This is me. It is real.

In My Heart

This heart of mine has led me with a divine intelligence that has been sublime. I could not have navigated myself to the shores of paradise without this wisdom of my heart, this inner compass where it seems the whole universe lives. Here inside my heart, I am guided toward the light. In my heart I see the holy star of Bethlehem.

I have found a deep and abiding equanimity here in my heart too. It feels like a gyroscope, always moving back into correction, balance, that sweet place in the middle. Always tender and easy. It's right here. That soft place in between the extremes. That middle, sweet spot, the secret place, the unseen refuge waiting for you to come inside. It's here, waiting for you. It seems to be felt and known through Love alone.

I am in bliss, moved by this honest beauty of divine secrets that continue to be revealed to me.

Even now, my heart never stops showing me what I need here in this ever-changing world of time. It shows me how to do what I need to do here in the world, here with you, here for you, here to give it all to you.

It shows me how to live in the world of constant change. I have awakened to the passionate moving energy and power of my heart. I smile. I love that there are no doctrines here in the heart of divine intelligence.

I feel exquisite love as my heart touches the holy Presence, the changeless light. This Presence will never leave or forsake me. How could it? It is my very Self.

This is my joy; my heart is in love with life, the very life of me, here, this one I am, as the light of God that I am. This is me, Life is me.

This sweet heart of mine will take care of me. My intellect used to think I needed reasonable and logical answers, but now, my heart tells me there is much more to this Infinite Ineffable God that is the All in all.

I know beyond a doubt God is all and I am the living of It. The words of St. Catherine of Sienna come to mind, "My me is God.... Nor do I see any other me but my God himself."

Nice going girl. You cracked the code. Live it, run with it. I've always felt a deep affiliation with the 14th century Christian Mystics. Most especially the women among them.

When this rush of beauty pours into me, I am imbued with this great joy and exhilaration that leaps into flames of wanting you, you wanting me, this tangible evidence of love made plain as you and I soaring in the freedom that transcends time and space.

Heart to heart, this mystical experience of Love comes deep into me. Here I find the resting place, the divine intercourse, the holy baptism. This, this living interface with life, leaves me breathless.

Love is brave. Well, it appears to be brave. Yes I am brave, but really, I just can't help but exhibit this love. It is impossible not to. I am not afraid, so I can't really be called brave. It pours from me. It is the Universe. Love is the whole entire Universe, and I can't help but be this Love.

In Love Always —

Pink Clouds

I laugh that I have become a bit like that symbolic Fool in the Tarot deck, innocent, spontaneous and looking upwards as I am about to step off the edge of a cliff. With wisdom, I know the drop is really only a few inches; I take a step and I am right.

I am filled with a sense of potential and adventure. I am free. I am seeing my world from the high pink clouds that float above. I'll take my chances and trust this power that has unleashed me.

Life and I are a fine pair. We are romantic and funny and we laugh. I find Life to be very amusing, with an excellent sense of humor, an intelligent sense of humor.

I'll jump in with joyful laughter and see what happens. I'll take that step. It's all beautiful, no matter how it might appear. It really is divine, made of something wonderful. It is the Light of God, no matter how I slice it. It's perfect because the Living Presence is All That Is. It is my pleasure to love and embrace Life's wild, untamed, ever unfolding bounty of experiences and appearances.

You and I, my Love, we took the Orient Express. The velvet and candles, carpets of plush indigo blue wool, tassels on the golden silk curtains, the rhythmic rolling and swaying of the train moving through the night, moonlight shining on the passing countryside. A bottle of wine, soft pillows and eiderdown duvet. Our warm bodies close, moving deeper as the lights flicker through the window. We don't know where we are going, and we don't care.

I am always yours —

Holy Mystery

Morning light sparkling through the trees.
Open bedroom windows, sweet fragrance,
Orange blossoms dance through the cool soft air.
Glittering golden sunlight awakens me.

Bounty and abundance pours upon me,
Runs over the edges.
I taste the honeyed nectars of Life.

How delectable to be the prize of this conquest.
How surrendered, revealed, giving I am to my victor.

I am the loyal friend, the faithful lover,
The deepest Heart of a Holy Mystery.

Feeling the exploding force of alchemy
In synergy with Truth and Light as it penetrates
My infinite beauty reaching the timeless depth of my soul.

For You My Love —

Scarlet Ribbons

William Samuel taught mostly through stories. It was a great way of teaching that worked well with me. Stories, like music, went straight to my heart.

William was giving a talk in White, Georgia, back in 1993. My husband and I were among a little group of people who had come to see him.

During the talk William told the story of an old song called *Scarlet Ribbons*. How the father hears his child ask in prayer for scarlet ribbons. Wanting to answer her prayer, the father goes out into the night to buy her some red ribbons. But it is late, the stores are closed. He finds no ribbons.

Then, sweet mystery of Love, in the morning there are scarlet ribbons laying on the bed of the young child.

Well, by the end of the story the whole group was in tears. Bill truly touched our hearts as the Child had been unloosened by that story.

Something stirred deep within me, and for just a moment I remembered the sweet little girl I used to be. She was pristine, credulous, bubbling with laughter, beautiful, alive, full of herself and she was awaiting my return.

Then Bill talked about death, he said to look for signs and wonders after a loved one dies, look for synchronicity, look for birds or lights or butterflies. He said the tangible evidence that our loved ones are still with us will show up for us in a way we will understand and know it is their spirit speaking to us through signs.

Bill addressed one gentleman who had recently lost his wife saying that Ruby was not really gone, that Ruby was right there with the man. He said that just thinking of someone is a way to bring them to us. Life, Consciousness, Awareness, Identity, which includes Ruby, does not die. That imagination is closer to Reality than the tangible forms are.

Bill added that if we watch and listen and if we are open to miracles, our loved ones who pass on will contact us in special ways to let us know they are not really gone.

I didn't know it fully at the time, but I had been transformed that weekend. Something happened deep in my soul. Something very powerful and very beautiful was awakened in me.

At the end of the talks, to my joy and surprise, William asked me to come up front and sit with him "to help answer questions," he said. I did the best I could. I was so honored and felt that Bill knew I was truly finding the Child and Its blessed gift of Understanding.

So impressed by what had transpired during the weekend talk that when we returned home I wore scarlet ribbons in my hair in honor of Bill and the Child that was coming alive again within me.

...But, here is how the story continues...

I jump now to three years later.

I was in my home, sitting on my living room floor, sorting a box of things to throw out. The TV was on. I was listening to Regis and Kathy Lee. It was a beautiful spring day, fresh and warm. The front door was wide open. The phone rang and it was Rachel, William's wife. Rachel was calling to tell me that William had passed away. I knew he'd been in hospital, so this was not completely unexpected.

I hung up the phone, adrift in emotions, sorrow, tears and love – knowing all is well, trusting what Bill had said so many times, knowing Life does not die, Awareness does not go anywhere.

When, praise God and behold...

I tell you the living honest truth...

After I hung up the phone, I walked back into the living room...

And I heard, coming from the TV, sweet and clear, Regis Philbin announce...

"Now, Harry Belafonte will sing that favorite song, *Scarlet Ribbons*."

Yes, there it was, the signs and wonders, the miracle, pure magic, the divine synchronicity. The Love comes to us in ways we can and do understand.

I knew this was a sure sign, a confirmation, no doubt about it, Bill telling me he lives! There is no death!

I soaked in the moment fully. I let Mr. Belafonte gently sing *Scarlet Ribbons* to me, tears running down my face.

I knew this was William's way of telling me honest and true that everything is alright and that I can trust and know the goodness of Life and that Love prevails.

Now, if you don't think this is wonder enough...

I cross my heart and tell you honest and true...

As the song ended...

Glory to God...

A bird walked in the front door.

A little bird walked right into the house. This little robin, it stood calmly, deliberate, with eyes sparkling, looking at me.

This bird was perfectly at peace and seemed assured of just what it was doing. It was about three feet away and it looked at me with its twinkling eyes and stayed for a few minutes. I kept holding to that little bird's gaze. We looked at each other, our eyes contacting each other. It was astounding. The whole room seemed to be glittering and sparkling in light.

The bird stayed just long enough to let me know that it knew very well what it was up to.

And then the little robin turned around, serenely, easily, confidently knowing exactly what it was doing, and walked out my front door. Did not fly, no, just very sweetly it walked right out the door and then reaching the edge of the porch steps it took off across the sky.

I had been given all the signs and wonders that day.

It was true, everything Bill had said and all I had come to know in my heart, was true. There It was, love and this tender heart of myself were entwined as Life Everlasting.

So it was clear. Life has no opposite. There is no death.

Now, these years later, many of my dearest loves have left my life in tangible ways, but I celebrate this Living Truth of God's Everlasting Light and Love every day.

Life is eternal and I know for certain Life and Love and all that we are, our soul, ourself, and the beauty and Truth of the ones we love will never die.

It's all still here, perfect and whole and right.

I have found the Child, and the Child has found Me.

You and I know it is true. You and all those you love are this Infinite Light that Lives as you and me and them. Everything is alright.

Trust and Love, you will see for yourself, you will.

I love you my Love, always and so very much –

Child's Science

"Awareness existed before any manifestation. Which is more significant awareness or manifestation? It is the Heart that instructs, not the words. The heart goes beyond words and cannot be fooled." –William Samuel

Awareness, Reality, Presence includes within It all time, past and future. All matter and form. Things seen and unseen. It is Infinity unfolding as this world we see and be.

One day I realized it was easy. I change the past by changing the present. I change the present by changing the past. It's all quantum physics. And it works.

Love really is all there is. It reaches from here to eternity. Love, it is a kind of Love that is unbound and lives as life itself, in and as all things. It is a stupendous love, a tremendous love of an Ineffable Isness that is being All that is and *all that I am*. It is this very awareness, this consciousness I am right here. It's Ineffable. I can't hold it, yet it's the wholeness of life and it is alive with all that I am. It's an Ineffable Isness that I call God. God is being all Life. It is the Love I am. The Ineffable is being everything that I see. It is the *basis in being* for every image, for every leaf, for every bird song, for every tender teardrop.

As William said somewhere, it is the joy happening underneath an apple tree, where every bee that buzzes is enraptured by the Love and Beauty. Every bee getting intoxicated by those rotting apples under the tree, is a joy to behold. What a fine joy of God we see as those drunken bees, those potted, smashed, inebriated bees partying on the fermented nectar from the fallen apples. And what a delightful story Bill tells about sloshed bees in the garden. I am enchanted by his humor and brilliance. I love the intelligent and charming way he teaches me how to live my own heart's knowing Truth.

This Love is everything. It is every swallow that swoops, every dog that barks, and my sweet lover, it is every kiss I kiss your tender, sweet body with. Beauty and Love. Love and Life. Sensuality, yes, sweetheart of mine, it's all so divine.

The Ineffable Love really is being all that we see and be and do in this tangible world. Just as there is an ineffable alphabet or the unseen principle of math, there is an Ineffable Source of

Life. Much like the spoken word, the intangible word, this Source manifests in and as the ideas made tangible. It is as if this world we see, hear, know, touch and feel is the intangible word made tangible. This world of time and matter is like the symbols, the letters of the alphabet. There stands a Divine Omniscient Principle behind the symbols. Therefore the Ineffable Divine Principle has its Being in and as all things.

This Divine Principle is the Love that is moving, living and being all things, every animate and inanimate thing. God the unknowable Isness, is just being about the business of being What It Is. It is Love *loving* and knowing Itself and knowing *what* Love is and *that* Love is.

That means that I am Love. I am the action of Love loving my world, loving the images, loving the people, loving the ones I love. Everything is here as the tangible Light of God. I see God in you, I am seen and known by God's Love for me, by me, with you. Love is known and seen and I see it now in all things. I see it in you my sweet Love. Life is the very action of love known and given, and lived, tangibly seen, felt, embraced in the form of the ones we love. And I love you because you walked into my heart.

How joyful it is to know you and to love you –

A Tendency

There in my enchanted cottage in Aspen I was thinking about the mystery of life. I looked up and out at the glorious mountains that were touching the blue sky, the aspen trees were dancing and twinkling in the icy breeze. It was all so lovely.

I could feel the Presence of God. God, the Unknowable Something that is the Source of all things. I knew God is the very Light and Life behind everything. But, I wondered how I really knew that? How did I know that this Ineffable One is All? How did I know there is only One Source from which all life arises? Did I just accept that on blind faith or did I really know? I did feel that I knew. But, how did I know everything is Mind, Light, Consciousness, this Living Totality of Being?

I recalled asking William those questions, and I recalled his simple, brilliant explanation. I had never forgotten his words. It went something like this:

"...All the philosophies speak of Oneness. Certainly, it seems to be the only thing that really makes perfect logic. When we consider life and look at the way things are, it becomes quite apparent that *everything tends toward oneness.*

"Everything we perceive points to this oneness. All things tend toward oneness. All of nature, all of anything comes from and goes toward oneness.

"Electrons and protons and other particles whirling around a single nucleus and it is one atom. And then, imagine, a whole passel of atoms and they wind up being one molecule. Yes, yes, back to one. And then we have a bunch of molecules that make up one grain of sand – beautiful, one grain of sand. Lots of grains of sand make one rock. Many rocks tend to be one mountain. And all nature, everywhere we look, we see everything tending toward singleness. And then we look and we see that many mountains tend to be one continent. Several continents become one earth. It's always a move toward singleness, toward one. Several earths or planets constitute one solar system – until we come to one final Universe and we call that God, we call that One Final One God."

I realized this really is true for everything. Everything always tends toward one. Many make one.

The *One Final Universe* is here, right here. I am the very Joy of Living Its Oneness. I am the very Life and Light of This One. It includes me and my little enchanted cottage, all of that was and is being the totality of Its Being. There is only One, and It is the one final and only single one that makes up the Totality, the Singleness of All That Is.

The One really is all this, the First and Last, the Infinite All, the Unknowable One. Clearly, the One Final Universe always existed and exists forever. This One called Godhead, the Divine Light, is One and always was and forever will be.

And, furthermore, I said to myself as I thought about all this, furthermore, since this God is all that is, then for sure, it is all this right here and now. This is the totality of life. Life *is* being the One and Only Final Oneness. How much more clear could it be? Certainly, that One Final Universe includes Life, doesn't it? Of course, because there is nothing outside of the Final One, It is the Only One.

So yes, it was obvious to me. Life right here and now is being this awareness that is aware. Life, God, the One Supernal One includes these trees blowing in the breeze and the crystal clear waters of my little Owl Creek and all those drops of water that make one little creek. That one little creek moves joyfully down toward the one big Roaring Fork River. And then that one big Roaring Fork and other tributaries all come to make one mighty big, single and only Colorado River. Thence that river and other rivers flow into the Sea of Cortez and out to the ocean, into one Pacific Ocean. That one Pacific Ocean's waters mingle and combine to become one entire sea surrounding and embracing the whole earth. One, it's always One. In One we see all that is. All things in nature always tend toward one.

And then I thought how Life, the one all-inclusive Total One included my little girls, my baby boy, my beautiful husband and all those mighty high and glorious mountains I could see from my porch. It included the birds that sang. Yes, the One Final One includes all the images of perception that are within the Universe. Everything, all things, all tending toward a single one. That which is being Life, *that* which is being things. That which I call God, Father/Mother God, the Supernal One.

Undefinable Why

William also answered this question: Why is *God* Ineffable? He said, because there is no way we can touch this Presence we call God. It is an undefinable term. It's impossible to say what this One Final One is. We can't put an outline around It because it is impossible to circumscribe Infinity. That's why words such as Isness or Reality are synonyms for God. God is impossible to define. We can define every *thing*, but no one, no one can say what God is.

William went on to explain that in fact there was a time in Hebrew history when the word "God" wasn't even written. They just made a dash or a mark meaning Isness. Because the Infinite All, God, is not a thing. Things are the qualities and attributes that make God "God." But God is not *in* the things, not *in* the qualities and attributes. Yet, God is Being All those qualities and attributes. God is being all things that make up the Universe. There can only be One, and it is ineffable.

Once again, my Heart was gently open thinking about all that William had told me.

In that moment of recognition of my Self, I was brought face to face with the Living Presence, right there on my little porch on that sweet fall day. I was so grateful to William for all he had shown me. I was there living the sweet mystery of Isness and I loved this beautiful world of mine. I was finding and living the Joy of Life I had been seeking.

Little did I know that all that wisdom and light would not prevent life's challenges. Life is ever changing. There would be some rough rides ahead, more difficult steps in this journey. I had not become fully free, not quite yet, but what I had found was the essential map that would guide the way. Little did I know I would be taken across the whole Sea of Life and shown beyond doubt the very knowing and living of true freedom, salvation and Life Eternal.

Wind Tossed Mystery

Oh I see my heart here, painted on the wall of an underpass, speeding down the freeway to wonderland. My wind tossed love. It's all about the brave, the noble ones, and the gallant ride of the fearless, unbridled Light of my heart. No one can catch her soul. She is the unleashed Beauty, wild and free. I hear the drums thundering power calling me. They beat with a gracious knight's powerful Love. Freedom. I hear the longing call of marching glory, shining bright on the hills and through the fields of purple and green misty haze. I run unbridled toward the sparkling ocean of my mind glimmering in the bright waters flickering the sun's sweet glittering light. I am freedom. I am alone in mystery and music. I hear the song and I am moved, spinning dancing to lyrical sounds of the winds of my soul.

I love you, my love —

Six
❦
Stormy Seas

When I was a little girl, on those rare stormy days in California, I would go down to the beach and stand on the cliffs above the sea. I liked to survey the pounding surf and feel the mystery of the dark ominous skies. Excited by the wild energy of the stormy weather, I loved the big, dark, silver-grey Pacific waters all churned in upheaval and turmoil. It was thrilling to feel the power of the huge waves slamming the rocks and spinning and turning, and seeing the ocean rearranging the landscape of the sandy shore.

It was all touching me, feeling me, and I feeling it.

And the sky was made of glory, yes, all mystical, moving and divine. The dark, wintery clouds were trimmed in radiant, silver gleaming white, as the sun's rays peeked through to create the beauty illuminating the grey clouds from within.

The sounds were a holy symphony singing pure elation to my soul.

Standing there in such powerful beauty, I would be enthralled with the majesty of it all.

I was a child. I felt life. I felt it all. I felt my body almost blown off the cliff. I was not afraid. My arms were stretched out wide to catch the ride.

The child was willing – no, no, more than willing – she desired to feel it fully.

My long hair, strawberry-blonde locks, tangled, tousled and windblown would be untied, sweetly touching my face, gently kissing my mouth.

Again, once again I feel such passionate joy. The child has returned to me.

I am the fearless beauty. She is alive and I cherish her for saving my life.

That little girl is here. She is standing on the high edge of Life, loving Life.

Now my heart and my arms are wide open. I am buffeted by Life. Like ever-changing weather I am blown this way and that. I stand open to it all, unafraid to fly off the cliff. I am called by the sounds, the songs, the music of the wind singing in my soul.

Vulnerable, revealed, my senses have come alive and I am watching the pounding surf of life which thunders below me and above me and within me. I am in love.

I am feeling that glorious ocean churning here in my soul. I am thrilled by the thundering surf, all in turmoil, the salty air that tastes like tears on my face. I am letting life reach me as I am reaching my soul.

The beauty of Life, so powerful and magical.

I remember lifetimes before this one. I remember when I stood on the cliffs above the sea on the lands of those ancient English Isles.

I remember the green fields I walked through leading to the edge of the wind-swept waters that touched the sky. I am blowing sideways, my skirts are like sails caught by the wild beauty, moving through it all. My soul is lifted high from the cliff and soars free.

There is a song the child hears. I am filled with its power and strength. It rushes to the depth of me, moves me, picks me up.

Now the storm passes and the earth is refreshed. The sun begins to break through the clouds. In this grey mystery the hard silver edge of light at the hem of the clouds begins to open to blue again.

The crystalline light beams turn golden and the sky transforms into the sweetest azure. I breathe the fresh life of renewed air and hear the sound of seagulls calling with the joy of freedom.

As long as forever, I love you —

This Is Real

I found the Child, the golden point where God and I touch close. The Child is the *Christos*. I was anointed, baptized with the Pure Consciousness of the Ineffable. It washed over me. Now, seeing both the real and the unreal as One. There is only One. The Christ-Child is the place where I meet in an interface with the Ineffable Love that is being this very soul of my Self. I found her atop the mountain, next to God — the Child. I took her hand and she has led me back down the mountain and back into the world where I have come alive and I live again. I have been resurrected, transformed back to innocence.

I am back in the world. However, I am not in the same world I left behind. I am in a new state, and yet a familiar state — a state of being, a state of mind, a state so lovely, gentle and easy, peaceful and real.

This heaven on earth is here with me. This, I have no doubt, is the heaven that Jesus said is spread upon the face of the earth that people cannot see. This is the serene Meadow that exists right here in the old world but it is hidden from sight. I am able to see it once again.

This, this is the real place. It is within, but it is seen, touched, felt right here as my world. This is the living sanctuary. This is a safe haven. This is peace.

After having my heart torn open, being stripped of everything I loved and held dear, I took it as an opportunity and let myself stand naked and bare and open to Life. After all, I had nothing to lose. I was willing and vulnerable and I just didn't really care what would happen.

And with that action, I saw the powerlessness of things, the illusion of time and death. Somewhere in scripture it says the last enemy to be destroyed is death. I got it. Now, I am free.

Many have walked through the fire to find themselves cleansed and resurrected by that fire. Some are willing to be humbled and purified by the pain. Yes, it is a letting go, a yielding, not to despair but into the arms of the sweet Ineffable. It is a yielding wherein relief comes and the guilt is lifted. The dawn of the new day comes when we are broken and on our knees.

Willing, asking to let Life show me the way, I saw the Light.

This was my journey Home.

This, for me, was my own true and authentic second coming of Christ, when the Christ arrived as wholly in my own heart, as the very heart and soul of me, as me, as myself. My savior came and it was me, my very self that saved me.

As esoteric and mysterious as that may sound, it's not. It is tender, simple and carefree. With this Holy Child leading the way, life is a joyful adventure. Nothing more. Nothing heavy. Nothing erudite or complex. No, it just feels like a sunny day, bright and fresh. It is a return to youth, innocence and wonder. There is now this sweet peace and extraordinary understanding that is based on a foundation of gentle, all-encompassing Love.

Hold my hand, come with me.

Paradise

I fell asleep last night to the sound of rain.
I was rocked sweetly by the holy melody of Love.
The soft song of midnight
Tenderly touching my soul.
Warm duvet holds me.
Thunder bursts and rumbles,
Pounding crescendos.
I woke up to Paradise.
It's like magic.
How Sweet this Life is.
I am astounded all the time.
I watch all this wonder unfold right before my eyes.
I love Life.
I Love the whole glorious trip.
It is simply divine.

I'll give what I can. I will do my best for you.

A Living Miracle, all of it. The deep peace of my soul touches Infinity.

I love sleeping with the window open when it rains. I love hearing the rain and feeling and inhaling the cold air of the scented garden, a bouquet of orange blossoms and jasmine. It touches me in the night.

As I want to touch you.

As I am feeling it all.

Life is sensuous. You know, now I live this sort of ethical, holy, divine elation, maybe. I am in love with the eternal light behind all things. My senses have come alive. I must balance all this passion that roars and thunders inside me. I must let it run and yet hold it near and dear. I live loyal and true to this sweet center of my being.

Wild. This is wild.

I can see that feeling such joy is feeling right up close next to God – the One and Only of My Life. Yet, as I live this intimate love with life, my world opens up to me entirely.

All of me is open, I hear the birds sing and the surf pounding and the flowers blooming and the colors dancing to an inner song of living love.

This song speaks to me with lyrics of light and beauty.

Late at night, completely unexpected, a noble knight enters. He bestows me with music in the midnight hours. He holds me close and takes me. I am his. The fire is lit. There is reason for this to happen. There is a divine destiny. Unexpected beautiful surprises come as I am wrapped in this lovers arms.

Life is the experience of God. The ultimate love affaire. I am in love with the very presence of life itself. It so happens the fringe benefits are mighty sweet.

It is all holy and divine. This world is alive and sacred. It is also romantic and very sensual for me, the way I love to be loved. Life manifests this holy Love in the tangible world. I am given the gifts of love. I am full of laughter and unbridled joy.

In the morning, after the rain, a gentle softness shines.

Everything twinkles with this radiant beauty in my eyes.

Where my heart is there is my love. And where my love is, there I see holy wonder in all the sights and sounds and images of God's living glory.

Grace has found me and yes, there was nothing I did to earn it. I have no idea why this has happened to me.

I am taken care of. I run free, right here in the Garden.

And you my sweet lover, your music fills my soul.

I love you always –

Deeper Into Intangible

"Throw away holiness and wisdom
and people will be a hundred times happier.
Throw away morality and justice,
and people will do the right thing.
Throw away industry and profit,
and there won't be any thieves.
If these three aren't enough,
just stay at the center of the circle
and let all things take their course."
—Lao-Tzu

You see, that's the whole thing. Having found this center point, this higher Self, this original soul of myself, I'm no longer subject to nor reliant upon the changing events and situations in the material physical scene. Well, yes, things may change, and they do. But, from this new position of freedom and fearlessness, I can let go of things and flow with the coming and going of Life. I can ride the wave and enjoy the ocean of Love that Life is.

Things may fall apart even, but nothing that is of eternal and everlasting value is harmed. Money can be devalued, things can be devalued, even people can be devalued, but what is Real is the one value that is always real, here, stable and factual – Life.

Love, Awareness and Life, the Divine Principle, remains Complete and All. God and Its all pervading Good are Real. That Divine Principle is the changeless value. The unseen things are the everlasting values.

The people, the soul, the life, the spirit, the love, the Isness of the people in our lives remain always with us – even though all things change. Even though we don't literally see them or they may seem to slip so easily from us, in Truth they are always here, always a part of what is. What Is is all that I am.

151

Just because we no longer see them in tangible form, that does not mean they are really gone. Life and the Light they are, the one they were and always will be, is always here. I know this, because the Presence is still here no matter where any *body* goes. Even if the body seems to die, the presence of life, the Awareness they are and we are is never not here.

Seeing things in this Light of Truth lets me love more deeply. I love my blessed world with all my heart. It is such magic to be experiencing Life – as I love you.

Yes, I can and do Love this changing physical world, and all the beautiful people who come and go within this seamless wholeness of my Self. My sweet world is really God Itself. There is nothing other than This.

Like catching a big wave, I just feel it, it picks me up and I am on it. When the waves come I can't turn back. I have no choice but to do my best and ride this. The flow of Life, like waves, never stops.

This is the freedom to be myself and live my heart's love right here in the world. Doing things my way, from the way I am shown deep in my soul and trusting this Light that guides me.

The purity and light of this holy transaction guarantees that you can take all of me, all my tender kindness, my heart, it's all yours. Why not? I don't mind. It flows through me. These vast waters of the divine Sea of Life flow through me. I am the living infinite flow of Eternity, of Holy Light, of Living Waters.

Living with my Heart exposed to everything, I can let you take all of me. I am the infinite wholeness that cannot be harmed, depleted or destroyed.

I guess – how can I say this – my Love originates from the cosmic explosion of infinite immutable power of the universe surging through me. It's ever present and it won't run dry, won't be diminished. This Love is forever.

Sweet Mystery I Live Your Love –

A Shining Star

I am a shining star. I needed to find this out for myself and the sooner the better.

One day I realized I had to accept my glory and my beauty. I had to stop rejecting my Light. And yes, so should we all know this to be true of ourselves and of each of us.

I walked up and I said, "I'll take my Life back now." God was very pleased with me by that demand.

This is my beauty and my light and my life that I have been given. It may all belong to God, but I am here to shine what God's Love is. I refuse to hide it any longer. God loves me for this bold and brave beauty I am.

I am confident. I am free.

I have finally come to trust myself, all aspects of myself. No images to live up to.

Broken is fine, bent is fine, stained, faded, whatever. I do not need to be fixed, or healed, or changed or live up to anything, I don't need to be molded in any way.

This is where I run free, as I am, unbridled I leap in joy. I am filled with the power and glory of Life, because I am, because I exist, here and now.

I have become my own Star of Bethlehem, leading myself back to the holy Child in the manger of my Heart.

Being filled with Illimitable Light, this Life Force electrifies me. I will shine this Light and give to my world and give to you. And I won't stop giving. I cannot help but give.

I will be a bright cosmic twinkle in the night sky shining the way home. I will let Life pour through me.

Not Buying It

Whatever this is, I am most definitely aware of it.

I've heard it said by some "enlightened ones" that if we know then we don't know. Ha! That's just not true. I am not buying it. It's not true for me, that is for sure.

I've also heard it said that those who know don't speak. I beg to differ. I have discovered God is good and God is the very joy of my knowing and speaking. Expressing my love and joy is irrepressible. A flower does not hold its fragrance back. A tree does not hide its fruit. Giving, it's all about giving. Loving this world, I must share this love. Having the words that sing to the heart and soul, this is my heritage. I am going to claim my power and beauty and live it boldly, no matter what "they say".

Whatever name for this state of being that has found me, I'll take it. I don't think I'd ever refer to this as enlightened – I would say whatever it is, I love it and I'll live It. This is the end of my search. I feel I am now at the beginning of a joyous adventure, simply living this sweet magic and watching what happens. If this is enlightenment fine – if not, I really don't care because I am free.

I am more than aware of this marvel that is blooming here in my heart. I am filled with lightness and laughter. I cannot deny what is here. It is running deep, like a river. It surges through me. It changed me. It moves me in new directions. It brings some marvelous surprises too. I don't know what is ahead on this river ride. I just ride it now.

It's as if I have caught a huge wave, as if I was in the exact right spot and a big wave just lifted me up. I had no choice but to ride it. To just give myself to It and ride.

It's been a most wonderful wave. It keeps going and it's not hit the shore yet.

I have also heard it said that no one can experience enlightenment because when we are enlightened the one experiencing is no longer there.

If that is true, if they are right, then this sweet place in my soul, the tender love I feel, this deep peace that has found me, this transformation, must not be enlightenment, because I am most certainly, truly, assuredly experiencing this. I am still here and I am absolutely joyful that I am.

Why would Life Itself not want me to feel and experience this sweetness of knowing what I am experiencing? Why would Love, God, Goodness, Intelligence not want for me to know and *know* I know, and feel all of it?

Actually, I think that is the whole point of being in this world, *the experience of knowing when we know.* To enjoy the excitement and wonder of learning, knowing, getting it. And to know it when we get it. To realize the lights went on. Of course we know. If we are in the dark and the lights go on, we know it. And then we also know the reason for the shadows.

Like learning to tie my shoes when I was a little girl. The joy was in the learning and then the delight in knowing. Learning to tie my shoes, yes, it was all mine. I got to know that I knew how. I was not deprived of that joy and thrill of knowing. Of course not. And with *that knowing* I could go barefoot and still know how to tie my shoes.

Why would the discovery of freedom, the finding of peace and the sense of being whole, be any different? It is a knowing and *knowing I know.* I am free.

Now, in the joy of knowing who I am, I know the joy of this sweet peace and happiness. I can skip and sing and dance in the thrill of knowing. If God manifests in my heart as my Father in heaven, that is wonderful. Who cares how God shows up? God is pleased and smiling with me.

I am bursting with happy hallelujahs and I am unafraid to shout them.

Whatever my previous concept of enlightenment may have been, it was not anything so wonderful as this. This is totally befitting who I am. How sweet that God knew exactly what it was I needed.

And another thing, this sense of equanimity has not taken my ego away. No, on the contrary, I am so much more myself. More, not less.

If this is illumination then illumination is Love. Loving Life and Life loving me. This knowing is experienced as vitality, strength, joy, peace, wonder, youthfulness and understanding. I am inspired, creative. And all this comes along with patience, kindness, security, comfort, openness and – well – there is so much more. Why would God deny me the knowing of these wonderful things, and *knowing* I know them? Well, He wouldn't and He didn't.

It is true, I certainly feel like I have been born again. I am this sweet, beloved spark of freedom that God has always known and loved and I get the joy of knowing I am this.

Whatever name it goes by, I am fully aware of experiencing it. And I don't need anything more than this – while yet, more seems to come. It's such a marvel.

This is Love, God is Love –

Love Grows

One spring day, when I was about 9 years old, I was given several large packages of sweet pea seeds. I can still see those big white envelopes of seeds, the package designed in colorful sweet peas on the front. I planted them, no I scattered them, tossing them freely along the fence on the side of the property at my mother's house. They sprouted and grew fast, they surprised me. Seemed as if suddenly, in just days, I looked out in the morning, and the whole fence had turned into a masterpiece of beauty, a living Monet.

The sweet peas had bloomed and they covered the whole fence in a gay, bright, colorful plethora of fragrant beauty. I had sweet peas galore. I inhaled all the perfumed pleasure of so heavenly a scent. The fragrance of sweet peas is like a dip into profound purity and bliss. The colors were astounding too. They were purple and lavender, white, periwinkle, light yellow, golden, every shade of blue, deep maroons, pale peach, every varying color of red I could imagine, there they were, from dark reds to ruby, to soft pinks and rich magentas. The bounty was glorious. I enjoyed those sweet peas that summer. I collected little bouquets of fresh flowers every day while they lasted. It seems to me they bloomed all spring and for a long time into summer that year.

I love sweet peas. I love how their curly green spirals hold them to the fence, how they hold on and they climb, how they hold tight to each other and grow into a bounty of beauty. They hardly last but a few hours after they are picked. They are lusty and yet so frail and delicate. Their perfume exquisite, their happy joy visible. I love sweet peas.

Perfect Love

Here is another wonderment of all this freedom. I don't have to be perfect. And, even better, I'm not.

I am perfectly happy about being imperfectly me. I love Life. I love my world in all its imperfect perfection. It is this: we are the living glory and beauty that includes all our sweetly imperfect perfection. I am imperfectly whole and holy.

This freedom lets me dare to try something and not worry whether I can do it right or well, or perfectly. I can at least try. I can do it my way, find out for myself. Make my own mistakes, learn from them. And that is a fine way for me. Even if it doesn't work, I find out, I know. I learn.

And now, I can do things that used to scare me. I surprise myself at how easy most things really are. I love the challenge of it all.

I am free to feel it all, winning and losing, catching the up-drafts and the downdrafts, blowing it, getting it, doing it well or not – unafraid. Here, in the wholeness, in childlike, untamed, innocent wonderment and joy – this is the freedom – because I know the true heart of everything *is* Life, and Life *is* Love and Love cannot be harmed. Love is perfect, always.

I believe in Faeries

My heart is filled with nursery rhymes and sweet summer days of Peter Pan the boy who kept ever shining bright.

The Child has the freedom to dream, to imagine, to love Life for all Its magic and wonder.

The Child can enjoy his memories of days gone by. The Child, the Real Self, that One is free to remember the past, to enjoy the romp in that unbound Love of memories, unhindered by time and space.

Here I am. What glory this is. I am here to fly, to soar, to reach the stars and ride with the fearless childlike freedom through the heavenly adventure of midnight's twinkling light.

Enchanted by faerie dust and glitter falling from the sky, I am taken to the secret Meadow where drifting bubbles' spinning pink and yellow rainbow prisms float across the azure blue.

I lay upon the purple blooms that carpet the earth. There I read aloud to you a tale of pirates and wenches and dark amber whiskey. I read to you of hidden treasures buried deep within the musty cool of earthen caves that glow in crystal walls of magnetic metallics and cobalts of lustrous beauty.

I tell you stories of the secret there, the jewels of radiant diamonds, sparkling rubies and glistening pearls to dazzle and delight your boundless depths.

I tell you of the green of emeralds that shine in reflections of the ancient hills beyond the sea where the winds blow free and the wild field of grass dances and sways in joyful rhythm of Love.

We can hear the siren's call, luring us across the sea, as she cracks the ship to bring those rugged sailors to their knees. As they tremble and fall under the spell of her captivating song.

The joy of the stories so delights you, sweet boy who holds my hand, your shining smile takes me with you. We go flying up and over the moon beam's silver road that leads across this glassy ocean of the living mind to where horizons never end.

I Love You, My Angel —

Forever With Me

"If you are willing to be lived by it, you will see it every-where, even in the most ordinary things." —Lao-Tzu

So, one day I simply leaped, realizing Life is all that I am. And in fact, God is all that is. What can harm me? How can I go wrong? And so I dared to let go — and leaped.

When I let go, life came rushing into that open space in my heart. It held me close and gave me everything and more.

Letting go, yielding to Life I found was really giving myself completely to accepting the Ineffable Totality of all that is. There the peace washed over me, the holy baptism was felt. Here I was anointed by the holy spirit, the Christ-mind poured over me.

Totality, what does it mean? Totality means everything is and always will be the very Allness of Divine Living Presence, the Divine Principle of all that is. Realizing Totality, I realized I was free — always had been.

Now I know I cannot let go of those I love. My loved ones are with me always. Totality is all-inclusive. That wholeness is who and what I am. It is who and what my loved ones are. Where can they go? What can be beyond Totality? What can be outside of wholeness? What can be beyond infinity? What can move past eternity?

It's all right here, and it's alright here.

I let life sweep me up in its arms and I let it take me tenderly to itself.

My child, my past, my future, my home, my things, my memories, my friends, my lover — you and me — all these exist always and forever, no matter how it might appear. The Truth is not changed, fact remains, Reality stands unaltered. Totality is total and we are that.

It turns out love is what Totality is, and God is this Totality being all that I am, all that you are. Totality is who I am and love is ever with me. Love does not go anywhere.

Life does not die. Love never dies.

The story of a love is not important, what is important is that one is capable of love, perhaps the only glimpse of eternity we can really know is when we love someone.

Love is the most deeply personal experience we can have. Love can only be felt in deeply personal ways.

It's quite lovely this whole thing. This lovely man shows up. I wonder who is he, why is he here in my life, what is he doing in my heart like this? And then I see, the inside is the outside. I know, he is love. Love is what he is, who he is, why he is. He is love. He may look like the dashing knight in shining armor, but he is love appearing like a man. He is love in the form of this dear man who wandered into my world. He is the process. He is the process of life, not the form, not a thing, not this or that, but the process that unfolds. And that unfolding is Love.

When I let go, I float, I am buoyant, and I can rest upon the living waters of life, like a little kid floating on his back in the in the swimming pool. This presence is here, always here. Like the water, it holds us. This is Love and it holds me and keeps me. It does not let me go, nor let me fall away or sink into the deep depth of the sea, no, now I float with ease in this unfolding Love, I rest upon It.

Love does not let us go – it lets us free – but it never leaves us. We are never separate or apart from Love.

I can't help but love you. I see I am the Universe and the Universe is Love. Love is unleashed and is who I am. I cannot help but recognize Love. It is the very Self of me. And Love is intelligence that understands itself. This I know.

I love you always and forever –

The Child Found

I soaked up every word William wrote. I could feel my heart open and a cool breeze of healing relief would come over me as I read. There was a Light in his words. I had found my way back to this holy gift of my Self. How very deep this goes now.

No one, no other author or spiritual teacher that I knew of, had brought up anything about the Child. But I know that this is the most remarkable, liberating and essential discovery if we want to live our authentic, heartfelt realization.

Eventually, little by little, I came to see for myself that every word he wrote, all he told me, was true. There is a Child within and It most surely Lives this divine interface, at the right hand of God. It is Real. I know what Love is. I know freedom. It is the Child of me that saved me, returned to me, came alive again to live fully the Joy of Being, both inside and outside as one.

William Samuel explained the flow of this divine interface in *The Child Within Us Lives!*.

"INSIDE/OUTSIDE, OUTSIDE/INSIDE, THE CHILD'S INTERFACE

"Nothing, absolutely nothing, is more important than the following: In all existence, there is a 'flow' involved. Be gentle with yourself and remember the flow of old. What was it? When we were children we interfaced with God and the world freely. Our imagination flowed without restraint into the world of people, places and things. By the same token, the world of people and things flowed freely into the child. We saw a frog (outside) and, presto, the imagination was off and running. Or, we thought of kings and queens (inside), and immediately the people walking up the street (outside) became part of the royal court (BOTH sides).

"Adulthood has woven a veil that hangs between the Child-heart and the world. The world outside has become the adult's reality, bound in time. The free-flowing exchange from inside to outside, outside to inside, has been interrupted and insulated by the unconscionable bastard we insist on being in linear time.

"Just as a stopped-up kitchen sink needs to flow again, it is necessary for us to regain the flow – outside/inside, inside/

outside – moving freely again. Examining one's own thoughts is the necessary first step – and make no mistake, it is necessary. The Child thinks differently than the old man, as you are feeling already while the Child comes alive in your experience. Of course, writing is not the only way to examine one's thoughts (and thinking), but it is the most immediate way to do it by one-self.

"In human history, the 'breakthroughs' to greater dimensions have inevitably occurred with writing playing a major part in the process – from the ancient forest wanderers to these final days of this civilization, as physicists sit pondering their equations. The historic Jesus may have written only in the sand, but who can dispute he caused much to be written? So, we do this writing for ourself alone – without an intermediary between ourself and God. Who stands between the thinking and the thought but our Self? In the end, all the words being spoken and written in the name of Truth are as nothing compared to our OWN experienced interface with Reality – inside and outside.

"The instant a word of our own is written on the paper before us, our tangible scene has been altered – moved toward darkness or light, for better or worse, by that written (and spoken) word. If we keep the flow passing between the heart and the fingers that touch the world, the old bastard's barrier becomes less opaque and our experience in the world starts improving. As the Child of us shows us our birthright atop Da Shan (and we're quickly on our way the moment we take pen in hand), the climbing adult diminishes, the Child increases in consciousness, more and more – until, atop the mighty mountain of Kwangse, naught remains but the True Identity, the Child I am.

"Despite all you have heard elsewhere, there is no way 'There' short of finding and living the Child that IS there and everywhere. There are no shortcuts. No church can take us there. No doctrine can do it for us. We may lay metaphysical claim to our heritage until the jade eggs of Da Shan hatch, but we don't receive that heritage until we BECOME the Child in conscious, living action.

"Intellectualism has its place, but it doesn't take us home. The Child's conscious 'return' to the peak of the mountain is accomplished in living fact before one gets off the temporal world's wheel of trials, tribulations, beginnings and endings, time and rebirth."

Something Else

"A man with outward courage dares to die; a man with inner courage dares to live."—Lao-Tzu, *Tao Te Ching*

Ah yes, now I can thank you for showing me something else too. I kept saying that I didn't know how I got here. I said I didn't know how I arrived at this sweet joy and abiding peace that has found me.

But you see, I do know one thing: I was very brave.

I took the journey and I walked right out. I walked away from fear, guilt, self-pity and blame. I walked straight into my broken heart, into the wide open heart of myself. And I did it without flinching.

Turning around, full circle, I walked back in, toward Me and I came Home to my Self.

As the brave, bold, heroic soldier, I was not afraid to die. I was not afraid to Live. I stood right there, face to face with Life and I let It take me. I stood there stripped, raw, forthright and willing to let Life take me.

Daring life to come get me, taunting It to show me what It could do to me. I had no idea what would happen, none. I had no idea if Life would lift me up or toss me over the cliff. I didn't care. I just did it. I bravely rode my fine steed into the unknown.

Just like the mythical ones, the gallant knight, the dragon slayer. I got on my fearless horse and I raised my sword and I rode right through the dark woods of my soul.

Why not dare? Why not face Life fully? I didn't want to live anyway, so why not see what Life is? What could it hurt? I had died already, so I had nothing to lose.

And then, on my knees, there in the wild forest, I saw my own beauty. I saw my radiant heart. Right there, in the dark woods I bowed to thank that part of myself that could not live up to my image of perfection, that idea I had carried so heavy on my heart.

The cloak of fear fell off in the darkness. And there, torn open, in the aloneness I thanked that part of myself that felt worthless, helpless and guilty. I thanked that part of me that brought me down. I thanked her for the beauty she showed me when I stood there in that radiant light.

I could see by contrast the power and reality of this Eternal one, of this Love and Wonder that was my Real Self. I found the unbound joy and peace. Alone, I found the Light. I could thank the shadow that led me to this sweet Light in the forest. I was shown the Light Everlasting, I was shown My Heart, My Soul.

Blessed be the dark forest that called to me, that said I must ride through it. Forced to ride, I had no choice. I knew if I didn't go, I'd be lost forever. I had to be the bold warrior, hero to the rescue of my own Soul.

There, in the woods, alone, I could thank the unreal part of me, the guilty one. She was never guilty. She is perfect, she is my beloved as well. She made the innocent, joyful real of myself visible. She led me here to bring me back to my Self. To show me the Kingdom is here within Me.

And so I thank the process, the whole marvelous process that I am Living. It was being torn open, getting down to the pits of hell, to be so helpless, that I can now see now, by contrast, the power and reality of this beautiful eternal being, this love and beauty and wonder of joy and peace that has become my very Life, my very Self.

I know now. I *know* that I know. I Live It. I live the living proof of it every moment of my days.

This is why we must take the full journey. All the way. Not stop, not turn around and not go back. Forge onward. Move on through and let the anguish bring us home to this sweet Light of abiding peace.

I am free and I can fly forever more. Free.

Love takes away the sins of the world, there is no guilty one. There never was.

In the light the shadow leads to the tree. There is only Love.

No matter which way you come towards it, it is always Love.

I love you my sweet angel –

Into the Mystery

When I first read this letter, I didn't realize the magnitude of what William was telling me. At the top of this particular letter, he had handwritten in red marker the word "Private." He would often ask me to hold his letters near and dear to my heart until I felt others could understand the true and deep meaning.

Yes, now I understand fully, this does feel like passion, wonder and completeness, just as William said. It is indeed nothing physical and yet everything physical. Oh yes, he had it all so right. His words are precious. I held tight the gift I was finding. This gift would one day take my hand, lift me up to where I soar now. And it is true, I have seen such exquisite joy and pain and wonder. Now, to find the Child of Me, untouched, unsoiled, unspoiled, sinless, guiltless. This is mine now. She is God's constant companion. It is the Real of us, each of us. There is nothing more beautiful than this.

"5/15/84

"Dear Sandy!!!!!!!!

"You are finding It. You are finding your Self. You are finding Me.

"Your letter of the 4th comes as a grand explosion, like a flowing Joy, like the entry into the Mystery.

"Hold it close to you. Don't let it go. It is virgin, pristine, pure, from the CHILD of yourself. From the Original Image, made in God's likeness.

"Whatever you do Sandy, trust that inner Guide that tells you so clearly – and praise all that has led you to it.

"Yes. It is too simple and wonderful and unbelievable for 'others' to understand (YET!!), so just hold it close and let it grow. It will stir your innermost being. It will feel like *passion* and *wonder* and *completeness,* like nothing physical, and like EVERYTHING physical simultaneously. It will bring such exquisite joy and pain and wonder you might question your sanity. All of that is I-Identity stirring. It is the Child of Me, the same Child of yourself – untouched, unsoiled, unspoiled, sinless, guiltless, GOD'S constant companion, the REAL of us...

"Do you hear what I'm writing Sandy?

"You are finding the Gift.

"It will be YOUR Gift to give to countless others, in the days ahead, soon to follow. If you trust me, watch and see.

"There are MORE wonders if you WANT to find them. You can find them under any circumstances. With a house full of kids, with a family who doesn't understand, with soldiers trying to kill you, with twenty friends coming to dinner, in the midst of the struggle It comes, effortlessly, DESPITE our efforts.

"You are a faithful lady, Sandy, so keep our words between just you and me, <u>please</u>. *Your letters addressed to me will be to me and go no further.* If they are addressed to Rachel and me, I will share them. You keep my confidences too, please, because there is much between us now. <u>I feel what you feel – and the joy/Joy you feel is mine</u>. These are things too personal and wonderful for others to fully understand as yet, so please be sagacious and wise. You know me most intimately now.

"I would like to send a copy of your letter to a suffering lady in New Zealand who is convinced that she will understand everything intellectually and no way else. I'd like her to see what me-sense surrendered allowed you to FEEL as you wrote your letter. May I? I'll give her your address and her's if you'd like to write to her. You needn't be intimidated by scholarly attitudes. You are finding IT – which is what all the world's study, at best, has HOPED for.

"One other thing: Sandy, let me know which paper or papers I have sent that has said something specific to you – or that helped you perceive what this letter indicates you've seen. This is so important to me at this time. If there is a date or title on the paper, either at the beginning or the end, let me know. I did not record which paper I sent to you. I followed my heart and just sent it.

"I'll await your reply SOON. Don't wait too long for time is of the essence on the world's scene. I love you gentle lady of New Light.

"Oh, how I love you tonight. Bill

"P.S. Because you have discovered you are not real, <u>you have become very real</u>. Because you have found that you have no value, you have become ALL Value – and more precious than anything in all the world. I LOVE you, my Sandy. So will everyone when they come to know what you've come to be. I drink your overflowing wine in thanksgiving.

"Send More!!"

What is interesting is that even when I reread that letter some ten years after he wrote it to me, I still did not grasp the depth of the ever-unfolding beauty this would be.

These years later, *now,* I do. Now I do. *Now I do.*

Magic Kingdom

"Earth is crammed with Heaven." –Emily Dickinson

Something like Avalon I suspect. Perhaps King Arthur and his dreams of Camelot are really his longing for this third place, the heavenly realms of the Child, our soul.

The soul is found again. Oh, the sweet Soul of us. Always with us, waiting for us to touch It once again. Yes, It comes back to us as we are simultaneously ushered into this sweet, abiding innocence of awareness. It is a living place where the childhood purity and state of being just slips softly over us. We are wearing it like a holy robe. It is magic and it takes me to a new world.

The Light is rediscovered and lived again. This time I live it knowing what I have been given. I know the treasure this Child is. My original state of mind is found again. But, it is not the same. Now I know that *I know.* This time around, I know what a sacred and holy gift this is.

169

I quickly realize I am not living in the same land any more. I am now living in a place that is just slightly, maybe a nanosecond, different from the world I was in before. And yes, I am still here in the world, but it is just not the same at all, and neither am I – not by a long shot.

Is this Avalon? Is this the magic kingdom spoken of in myth and fairytale? It certainly does seem to be. It is a real place right here in the middle of this chaotic world. It is real and fresh and rich and new and alive. As I live here in this kingdom of the Child's Light, It keeps me vital and energized and full of joy. Clearly, it is not the same world I left behind. Clearly, I have found some strange and wonderful place in the midst of the old world I used to know.

"Heaven is spread over the face of the Earth and men see it not." But, when we find the Pure Heart, the Pristine Eyes of Love, we do see It. Yes, it all comes clear.

This world, all around, it is Heaven, right here as I live and love and laugh.

That seems to be the unbridled delight of this Child's state of being, sweet and fearless, soft and open. My world confirms my Heart's knowing visions.

Yes, fairylands and Avalon and the noble Knights of the Round Table. It's all true. Amazed by it all. Sailing is easy and smooth, a gentle breeze blows here. My sails are aloft and they catch the wind's sweet breath of kisses – and I take off for new lands and wondrous adventures.

I love you and you know I do –

Progression of Awakening

My favorite book by William Samuel, *The Child Within Us Lives!* charts the way to return to our carefree Original Nature.

"The progression goes a little like this: One searches and thinks he has found – and grows arrogant in that finding for a long time, thence to be humbled.

"Then, he finds again and really knows.

"One lives this discovery and proves it.

"One keeps going onward and finds the relationships between himself and the outside. Many people never reach this point because no one has told them or convinced them there is a relationship between the inside and the quantum outside or that these two are a single one.

"One perceives the wholeness of outside because he has found it for himself.

"One perceives the relationships between himself inside, and the appearances outside, in their increasing detail. This has been called the web of interrelatedness. A leaf falls to the earth and the universe is shaken.

"One comes slowly to know the marvel that will unfold outside from what has already unfolded within himself – and he lives in continuing expectancy of this unfolding in the world.

"One speaks to his world as seems best.

"All along this progression, one is faithful to those who have been given to him. He tells them to go and do the same and instruct their given to do the same.

"We, and those who have been given to us, become the New community, the flower of the tree of life. The Community grows.

"This progression happens in linear time, 'line upon line, precept upon precept, here a little, there a little.' "

Seven

In the Stars

Let yourself be happy with you. Begin loving you for your own beautiful heart that you know so well.

You know your own soul and your tender love.

Just love you for how brave you are. For the Love you are. For the Light you are. For the heart and soul you are.

Love yourself for the broken and lovely totality of your heart. For your broken heart, your tears and your sorrow.

It is all written in the stars. You are the Light and Life of the Infinite Celestial Love. You are the Timeless Child watching yourself reflected in time.

You are the Music of the Spheres, the chords, notes and melodies, the pull of your heartstrings, the boom of Love in your Heart, the sound of the Universe, the harmony of your song.

Love your Self as the Jewel of Light and Magic that you really are. Even when you don't know It – It knows you.

Begin tenderly caring for that sweet child light that you are.

As you do, she gets bolder, she gets sassy. She comes forward and says, "Take my hand, I'll show you how."

She stands up and says, "I'll lead the way."

And she does.

And it is a love affair between you and Life and your heart and soul.

You will recognize this unbound Child, she will be so real and familiar.

You will fall in love again. In Love again with your own Light.

Let my words be a love song to you from yourself.

As long as the stars are above you –

No Wrong Turns

My wrong turns turned out to be right turns when all was seen from the top of the mountain. There are no mistakes.

As the guy who invented the engine said, "Start her up and see why she don't work." I don't know about anyone else, but I assume it is the same with most of us, my mistakes have been my biggest and finest teachers. It was by seeing what is not right and what does not work that I was led to what is right and does work.

Now I rarely see many things happen that I would ever call a mistake. I think I don't even know what a mistake is anymore. Suffice it to say, I have learned how to live free and easy realizing nothing is ever a mistake. Mistakes teach me. Or, essentially, mistakes are good. If mistakes are good, are they mistakes? Or are they instructions?

"The day I thanked my suffering was the day it ended," said William Samuel.

The unexpected pleasures of this love affair with life keep unfolding. I am living it all, sweet and easy. Life is showing me how. I know it happened by divine destiny aligned aright – Life does that. It is the mystical synergy. Powerful forces of Life have brought me to this wonderland that keeps revealing to me these sweet gifts, these joyful surprises.

I'll take it. I can do it. I am ready for the twists and turns too. This is a wild adventure. I will ride this beautiful stallion.

It is as if the angels just swept me right into this new world and showed me the way to do what I need to do while I am here.

But, really, abandon the concepts of what you think being "awake" might be. Let it all go and then you will know for yourself. You will be in touch with Its profound depth and then you are going to be totally enchanted by what transpires.

And then, when I speak of all this, I get such a rush of love for you. Let me kiss your sweet lips, because you were a most unexpected perfectly fitting piece of the puzzle. This open way of living always provides exactly what I need. It provided you. That is very clear.

Now, let me kiss you. Let me love you and enjoy the ride to wherever it is I might be going.

Yes

Yes is perhaps the sweetest word of all.
Yes, I will.
Yes, my love .
Yes, I love you.
Yes, you are beautiful.
Yes, yes, yes, let's do it, let's.
Yes, why not?
Yes, I see, I see what you are saying, yes.
Yes, come hold me, hold me close, hold me deep, yes.
Yes, my love, everything is alright.

So he said to me, You are charming and energetic. I am falling in
love with you. You are fun, you make me laugh.
I said, Yes, you too. You do that to me too.
He said, I like that.
I said, Yes, I do too.
He said, I love that feeling of harmony and peace you have. I can
feel it touch me and it moves deep into me.
I said, You are unpredictable and powerful. You are a force of
your own, my dear.
He said, You are always enthusiastic, kind and optimistic.
I said, I think neither of us would say no to an adventure.

Balloons

Whimsical, the word is whimsical
I am painting a whimsical piece for you.

I have become the teenage queen —
Dream on – dream on –

Wild, untamed girl of my childhood
Has returned to me in all her beauty.

You and I can lay under a tree
And watch the sky
While the big magenta sheep
Eats the daisies and wildflowers.

Love, it is all about love
Everything is beautiful
I have no fear, I am undone.

I have no tethers on this balloon of mine
My balloon soars free and I am in love with
The sky, the sun, the fields of gold, the hills of green.

Come, let's climb in, you and I
You can light the flame, you heat the air
Our balloon will go up and up and away
Drifting through the sweet bliss of untamed innocence.

Pilot to co-pilot – Looks like clear weather all the way.
Co-pilot to pilot – Yes, captain, I see that.
Pilot to co-pilot – Do you trust me?
Co-pilot to pilot – With all my heart. I'll take what comes.
Pilot to co-pilot – Good, then hang on – here we go.

Glimpse an Idea

I opened another letter from William. I would come to see his predictions were right on target. Yes, I had lessons to learn, I had more to do, I would find my way, I would find the Child and Its simple unbound Joy.

"February 25, 1985

"Dear Sandy with the children and noise,

"You've had a Glimpse of the Idea and it won't ever leave you.

"About children: We are children twice. The first time we are child-children, like yours – running every direction, unaware of the world and its difficulties.

"Then we are adults, filled with woe and anguish, wonder where the Child within has gone.

"Then, a rare few of us — you among them — become aware of the Inner Child again, to slowly, surely BECOME the Child the second time. What for? To be able to tell the rest of the husks who have buried the Child within themselves and think it's dead.

"Sandy, within a few years, your knowledge of the Child within will be a saving grace in the world. Learn your lessons well. You have quite a work in store for you.

"You are much loved,

"Woodsong atop the hill, Bill"

The Lawn Swing

Remembering years ago, growing up in Southern California, life was full of fresh air and sunshine. I spent much time outside. Everything in my world seemed to be teaching me. I was a good student of Life. I was not so fond of school, but I was curious and interested in things. I loved reading. I adored spending time at the library with my mother. Learning was natural to me. I was listening and observing Life and its mystery. I also felt a great aliveness in me. I was observant and had a mind of my own.

As a little girl, I enjoyed sitting on the lawn swing with my mother on summer afternoons. Whenever we sat out there together she would play this game with me. She would be reading and she would say to me, "Close your eyes, and open your ears. Now try to find all the sounds and noises you can find."

And I would do that. I would close my eyes and open my ears and be so quiet, so still — and I would listen. I would listen to it all. I could hear the gentle creak of the lawn swing. I could hear a car door slam somewhere in the distance. I heard far away voices of people talking, a songbird singing, the bark of a dog and the screech of a hawk soaring above. I could hear the buzz of a little bug near me and the rustle of the wind in the leaves. Listening, I could hear the distant ocean waves breaking and traffic moving on Coast Highway. So quiet, ears open, scanning like radar, I would listen, listen with my whole body, searching within every strata and all the levels and dimensions my perceiving could take me to. I could hone in on so many sounds, at various distances. I was fascinated by the game, seeking to find as many sounds in the stillness as I could.

Now I think back about those times on the lawn swing with her. She covered a lot of good parenting in that one little game. She was always a very wise woman and a good mother. Maybe in her own clever way that game kept me quiet so she could read. To me it was brilliant. I hope in her next life she is enjoying her beauty and experiencing her wonderful self, as she is. She was a genius with a mercurial mind. She was wild, poetic, capricious and moody, she needed to run and dance and sing and be free.

She showed me how deep this world is and gave me my freedom to find the magic that this world is. In her game of listening, and in so many of the gifts she gave me, I learned to open myself up to Life and be free.

She was a gift to me. I am grateful she was in my life. I will love her always. She loved me, she trusted me, she gave me wide open spaces, she gave me plenty of room to live it my way.

The View Changes

On that lovely brisk fall day, I continued to read William's letters. I see now that nothing can be fully understood without the return to the transcendent Eternal Light of my Self, the Child I Am. It doesn't matter how you get there, how your Views change and expand, it all comes down to reclaiming the Child you are, your Original Self.

"October 21, 1985

"Dearest Sandy,

"I've been remiss to answer your beautiful letters. Please forgive me. It has been a turmoil here — editing and the like. You can imagine. It's been like a house with twenty strange kids tearing around — and you know a little about that.

"Lovely Sandy, you are getting it straight. You are doing it just right. All I could possibly add is small compared to the Light you are seeing. I would tell you that the View changes, expands, grows — and what seems a final answer today becomes the groundwork for a grander answer tomorrow. Sometimes it seems like a falling away or a coming home, but it is always GOOD going on no matter how it seems. Those who are given what you've been given are few and far between in the world. But those who HAVEN'T been given it, exist within our View. Which means it is up to us to help them see. That's what keeps me here sitting before the Rabbi's keyboard, whapping away with words and feelings.

"The FEELING is the thing, Sandy, as much as anything else. The feeling of Love. Do you understand that? We aren't to be fooled by the pictures, but UNDERSTAND them.

"Tell me about family? Tell me about the kids. Don't worry about your words or how you write, just WRITE. The world is waiting for You.

"I love you, lady of Light"

Looking for Good

Must have been the Saturn Return or perhaps a sharp bend in the river of life. Maybe a twist in the tapestry of the fabric of time. I really don't know. But there seemed to be this slippery shift in our lives there in our Aspen home. After twenty-five years of pure sweet perfection living in paradise, a feeling of change began to stir. It felt uncalled for and unwanted. Was it planetary influences, the stars causing upheaval? I don't know what brought it on, but it all felt uncontrollable, like the weather. It seemed as if a great storm had blown in and it wanted to blow us away.

As the storm blew we stayed close, we did our best to batten down the hatches, but nothing would hold this storm off. Our little fortress of perfection began to tumble down.

It's really just life, life is not static, nothing stays the same, but I wanted everything to stay the same. I did't want this to change, not ever.

I may have once been a brave and sassy young thing, but now, no, I was not good with this change that was uprooting us, blowing the lids off. Though, I knew things change, I knew there was something intrinsically good about these changes, I didn't want any of it to change.

After much desperation trying to save it all, the fates tore it all from us.

We sold our beautiful home, we packed up, we moved away.

It was a strange time. Out of decisions that seemed to have been made in the fog of a confusion that was cast over us like a mist, we found ourselves buying a rustic, rough, neglected little home in a small town in the mountains of San Diego, California.

It was a long, long way from our sweet Rocky Mountain paradise. Our Rocky Mountain high was over. We were in a new land and a new life. I felt entirely lost. It was another world compared to our beloved life and little home in the valley. All that was gone, all of it. We were never again to see our dearly loved, sweet, country home by the creek.

Something about life that just takes us places we had no plans on going to. Something about life sweeps us up whether we like it or not.

I was looking for the Good in all of this. I knew it was there some place.

Choosing Good

I had no choice in the situation. I did, however, have a choice as to how I felt about it all. Attitude. It was going to be all about my attitude. I had to live from my heart and soul, and from the highest order of things. I had to give myself to everything. That's where the magic happens, in the spirit, in the soul as we live the Divine Equation of giving and receiving

I coached myself. I figured *God is good* and *God is all there is*, so what could be bad? How could it not be just as good here as it was there? What's the difference? Since Life is still here, since Life is this Living Presence, then Presence is still here and I am still living this Presence wherever I am. So be it. Nothing really changed, only the scenery had changed.

Since I knew all this light of understanding that flowed to me had to be tested and proven by me alone, I decided to make the whole crazy situation joyful, a new adventure.

I would take the tangible action to make wherever I was a loving haven for us. I would walk my talk, practice what I preached, *live* this Love that had come to be seen.

Everything is in the mind, inside of me. It is all about what we think and how we react to those thoughts. It is about our state, our attitude. Really, it is about who we are and how we *be* who we are, how our intention, our perspective, is lived.

I trusted myself. I knew my wisdom came from a higher Source. The heart knows how to live aright no matter where I lived. It would make no difference where I lived, the Truth does not change. No matter where I am, there is love. Love is within me. The Presence of Life is present anywhere, everywhere I go. I take me with me. I am the Light and the Love. If I am happy and feeling love then wherever I am *everything* feels happy and in love. It's a state of mind. That's the whole amazing miracle.

Therefore I would love this new world we were in, and love it all into the beauty I felt inside me. Everything is pliable, everything is mystical, everything is made of mind, of consciousness, of spirit and light. I would not settle for less than seeing love and beauty here in our new home.

It was very clear I could feel love no matter where I was or what my situation. It was up to me. I made the choice. I knew love is always available no matter what the circumstances. It was all in my hands.

I chose to rise up, stay with love, stay with life and light – and so I did. I had to put it to the test. I had to prove my own true heart – and so it was and so I did.

Poetic Justice

In this new town, in this new home, my desire was to create beauty. And this new place we found ourselves in was quite beautiful – strange – but beautiful. Old oaks covered the landscape. A large pond and a huge barn with a stone foundation sat on the land. We had fresh spring water that came from our own well. I could feel a kind of holy mystery that painted the acreage.

The spirit of something magical from the roots of old California could be felt. There was nothing but nature around us and that powerful spirit oozed out about this place.

Although we had to adjust to the solitude there. Destiny had brought us to a kind of sanctuary of quiet living. It was like being stuck in a way station on my way to the unknown. I felt isolated and alone. I couldn't go anywhere on the spur of a moment, there was no place to go. I couldn't escape, run to town, go shopping, buy something new. There were no friends. No, there was nothing to do there. No place to go. No jumping in my little Audi to go for breakfast with my husband at Pour La France. No, no going to the club for tennis or dance classes. No lunch with my girlfriends at Ute City Bank. No skiing. No Friday nights out, dinner at La Cocina or Poppies Bistro, Little Nell's, or Farfalla. No gorgeous shops like Pitkin County Dry Goods, P.E.101. No indulging in beautiful clothes to buy, to acquire something to make me momentarily happy. No, just me up against the quiet and nowhere to go. Nothing to do but be where we were, alone in the California backcountry.

So, what did I do? I did everything with good intention. Every day I lifted my heart to see the light and beauty in everything. Good practice.

I'd wake up every day in that strange new place and let my heart be just sweetly and happily in love. It was a deliberate choice. I wanted to wake up to a new day and a feeling of knowing everything was alright. I felt that to be in my loved ones arms would be the kind of love I wanted reflected there in that new home. So I loved my husband first. Then I loved the days. It was all about the energy, the spirit, the feelings. I knew kindness and affection was powerful. I knew I could look out and see love, see beauty and see peace if I was feeling love, beauty and peace. In my soul, in my mind, in my heart, I could see God's glory in all that is and all that I am. If I made that choice to live in the Light of the Presence of Being then I would see Its tangible evidence.

Although it was a difficult change, I made the best of it. I enjoyed the pleasure of that sweet land and the silence of nature. I used the quiet time sitting on the deck overlooking the big pond, writing every day, writing in my journal, writing my heart out.

And I was reading, reading a lot, it was quite heavenly. I read all kinds of spiritual, metaphysical books, including Bill's books. I would write my latest insights and my deepest understandings. I could no longer write to William, as he had passed away about two years earlier. I was writing to myself. I was *Journal tending*, as Bill had called it.

Our daughters were off to universities. My eldest was at Wellesley in the east and the other was at Boulder in Colorado. Our son was still young, only 13 years old then and there was no school that I would let him attend around there. Homeschool it was. I loved having him around. He was so sweet putting up with all these changes. Being a wise child, he took it all very philosophically. But more, he was a truly good young man. Having had such a devoted dad in his life, our son had the fine character and noble qualities of his father, as did our daughters. He made the best of things. He learned to drive the old tractor that came with the property. He took flying lessons at the local airport. He did his homework all by himself. He did just fine.

For me, it was as if Life had sanctioned me to a mysterious monastery in the hills. All I could do was keep my heart in the right place, be with peace, with love, be tender. And so I loved my husband, I loved my children, I loved the land, I loved the mystery of Life and I loved my way through it all. And all the more I loved myself, I was finding that one I'd lost years ago right there within me, as my very own soul.

Interior Design

"If you want to know me,
Look inside your heart." –Lao-Tzu

Yes, and the funny thing was that putting this Light of Truth and Beauty to the test showed up for me as redecorating.

That house was a perfect living metaphor. The outside and the inside "shall be the same." As painful as this upheaval was, I had to keep my own interior, my heart and soul beautiful. This needed to be reflected objectively as a lovely home.

Literally, I did some major interior decorating. I created a home that reflected the divine chambers in my heart. I made beauty and love visible in my tangible world. And, as my heart was, so was my home. I made that house into an artistic bit of loveliness, goodness and warmth.

Inanimate things do have spirit and life and intelligence. This I know. And maybe only because nothing is outside of the living awareness that is being all things, all images, all tangible life. Things are made of light and light is information, light is carrying information. Well, whatever it is, I know everything is conscious and responds to love. Love is the answer. Love is always the answer.

In order to make the house feel like my soul, I used a lot of colors, rich deep reds, earthy taupes, and the almost-black of a dark forest green. The high beamed ceiling I draped in baroque wine-red damask, with subtle angels woven into the silky fabric's texture. English florals in cabbage rose mingled with tassels and silks. I gave it all an elegance mixed with an exotic, subtle and unobtrusive, yet romantic feel. Every room became sublime.

Now we had cherry wood floors for our bare feet to enjoy in the kitchen. We also had the great pleasure of cutting a large hole in the wall of the bedroom and put a big window in. Then the closed-in dark of that room turned to light. It was shining beauty, open to the fresh air. Bright fresh freedom came into that space. Remodeling was all very good.

Morning's twinkling light was beaming through the ancient oak trees outside. That sunlight now danced its rays into the bedroom. And through the big window we could see the starry sky at night.

It turned out the land in the California hills was exactly where we should have been. There was something on that land that was very conducive to transforming me. Although I would never have asked for any of it, it turned out to be just what my path required.

I felt I had to be willing to go through this, and trust it all.

I was right.

Oak trees and their acorns are a symbol of transformation, and I saw the meaning of those trees and took them to heart. They were my friends all that year.

I was breaking away from my old concepts, former beliefs and misconceptions. Misconceptions even about my beloved studies of the Absolute, non-dualism, metaphysics and God. I'd not yet fully understood the whole vision. But now, now I was setting myself free. I was opening up into *Something Real,* something vital and alive about myself. It was absolutely reliable. I was finding my Self, returning to the Child, the holy Child, the original Child that William told me I would find.

Wild Horses

I remember the day I found my freedom again. I was walking down a quiet, abandoned dirt road there in the San Diego hills. Along the side of the road was a meadow, a pasture with a herd of horses. There were perhaps twenty-five horses grazing quietly on the green grass in the late afternoon light.

I stood to watch them, enchanted by how lovely they were. Each in their own diverse coats of colors glistening in the late low sunlight and shadow; golden, mahogany, black, dappled, and pintos, whites and chestnuts.

As I was silently watching them and admiring their beauty, suddenly the whole herd just bolted. They took off in a thundering, wild, galloping, prancing, running, manes flying, hooves kicking, pounding, untamed, sensuous, joyful, spirited dance of leaping, unleashed freedom, across the field.

Wild -- Just Wild and Wonderful.

The rush of energy went deep to the core of me. The Power just ripped me open. The feeling pounded me, thrilled me, lifted me, shook me and woke me up — as if those horses had run right through me and blew me open, blew wide my heart — shattering me into pure Joy and Praise for the Magnificence and Mystery of Life I was so privileged to witness.

I knew it then. I heard this voice deep in my soul say to me, "Sandy, be yourself, I love you as you. I love you as the wild, untamed, unbound, sparkling, laughing, tender heart that you are. You saw that, you saw yourself — now, go and be what you are."

That was it. I did see It. Myself, me, my spirit, who I am — I saw myself in those horses. I mean, I really saw my Self. That was me out there. That was who I am. That was my soul, my spirit. Those gallant, powerful horses showed me who I really was. I remembered my spirit. I remembered Her. She was still here, and she was me.

I realized that all along I had made a major mistake. I had been trying to eliminate "me" in order to be free. I thought there was some part of me that needed to be nullified, annihilated or restrained. Now I saw it was quite the opposite. I was to turn around and return to myself, love myself.

From that day forward, everything changed. I came back to my Self. Slowly, at first. But I knew I was being transformed. It was clear. The Beauty I saw that day was so familiar, she was my Heart, my love, and she was easy to reclaim. I had been her once and knew her Soul. I wanted her back.

I see now her Soul sits next to Reality and I can trust this Self of Me. Those horses brought me back. They brought me home. I was free. I came alive again right there on that dirt road alone with the horses and nature and God.

The Unbound Beauty I saw in those horses was the spirit of me, the Self of me, the one that God, Life, knows me to be, the one *before the world was,* the Child I am. This was sweet bliss. It was all about finding myself, not getting rid of myself. It was so clear. Yes, I had always been this wild beauty, fearless, on the run, galloping in pure freedom across the Meadow of this blessed world experience.

Finding my Self I found Peace and Love. I came alive, I found myself. I fell in Love with Life again. I remembered me. I love me. I feel like a little girl again and everything has become sweet and easy.

Now the Magic happens all the time. It is Life Itself. As I Love and embrace Life evermore, the more the Magic unfolds.

Like those wild horses, I was free, already. Each of us is the whole, divine, individual and I am the way back to Life – just as you are for you.

Through my Self, I come home to peace and joy. Through me, not away from me. By way of me, by way of this identity, I find God, I find tranquillity.

There is an Original Self. It is who you are. It is made of holy stuff. Just as I am, there is nothing to change but only to uncover and unleash.

Love and let the Magic begin.

I love you –

Blooming

"The privilege of a lifetime is to become who you truly are."
—Jung

Here in the hills of San Diego something remarkable was happening to me. I began to rediscover myself, the Child. The Child that, years before, William had told me I would find. I was blooming and letting go as I bloomed. I was taking the old layers off. The little girl I had thought was lost to me forever, she was being slowly, ever so slowly, revealed to me and returning to me.

So, it turns out our year "in exile" on the land in California was the perfect place for my undoing and renewing.

Now I could see the Truth was not about becoming like God, it was about unleashing my heart, uncovering and claiming this authentic Self of myself, the heart and Soul of Me that God loves and knows. It was about knowing and living the Truth that God really is all that is, that God, the Ineffable Something, is the presence of all that is.

My feelings, my senses, began to come alive again too. I could feel everything. I could feel this excitement stirring in me. I could feel this joy bubbling inside, filling me up, spilling out. I felt like a little girl again, in love with my whole world. I was uncovering the Child, the Sweet Light of my Self.

The prophets have, nearly every one, spoken of a mysterious Child and childlikeness to prevail in the end days of linear time.

"For unto us a child is born, unto us a son is given: and the government shall be upon his shoulder; and his name shall be called Wonderful, Counsellor, The mighty God, the everlasting Father, The Prince of Peace." —(Isaiah)

SANDY JONES

On the Move

We'd been in that kind of monastery world nearly a year and we both knew it was time to sell the place, time to move on.

I had made the house seductive and appealing, just as I was beginning to know how very powerful and unusual I really was.

As much as I had grown more beautiful so had that house. It was impressive what we had done with it. I was confident that we had composed a place anyone would want to buy.

Reading the local papers, I could see most homes on the market were not selling. I was a little worried because I so wanted to get out of there.

We went for it anyway and raised the price from what we'd bought it at, adding in all the renovations and updates, all the new appliances and our time, paint, hard work and decorating expertise. And within a few weeks it sold to the second couple that stopped by. We sold it to a well-known author and his wife, a charming young couple who loved what we had created.

I had walked through a year of seclusion in wonderland and done it with honest integrity. No matter what the changes had been, I never left the light of love, joy and grace. I clearly had choices and I chose Love.

Life brings us all kinds of changes, events and situations. I felt I should, I could and I must live those situations from the very deepest, purest sense of my own heart's understanding. Life gives us the chances to do things right. This is where the power is. It is here inside of me, within my soul, always with me. My journey, I realized, was all about Identity, all about who I am.

I love you my Sweet Love, always –

190

Beloved Reality

"Forget not that the earth delights to feel your bare feet and the winds long to play with your hair." –Kahlil Gibran

Life calls to me to come in and ride a wave or two. I want to ride a big wave. I want to catch that monster breaker and take that sweet, rolling wall of water all the way.

Playful, life is playful. It says, "Hey child, come and get me." Life says, "I am here for you to take me, catch me and ride me all the way." It says, "Come to me, let me be your beloved, your teacher, your friend." That's what my sweet Life says to me – when I finally listened.

I opened my heart, I expanded my vision. I let all of Life in, letting it come into me, allowing Life to use me. Knowing now this journey was between Life and me.

Yes, I was transformed. Or should I say I was returned to myself, to be the unbound, holy, original little girl I used to be. This time, knowing what is Real and exactly what is *powerless* as images within this Reality.

Life is powerful, like a huge wave in full force I can feel Its unrelenting love.

Like waves in the ocean, life doesn't stop coming. It is a day at the beach. It is exciting really. The whole marvelous explosion of pure energy, a surfing adventure, seeking the big one, the endless summer. The joy of understanding.

This is what life is. This is the beauty and magic.

It is a two-way street. Life has this desire to take me, love me, enjoy me. I will give into It now. I will trust Its love and give It my all.

As the Child, incorruptible and holy, I am here once again. I am here to *live* and enjoy the beauty of every moment, every day.

Life is my wave. Life is my teacher. Life is my beloved. And It does a fine job with it all. Nothing can hurt the one we really are.

No, I don't want to miss this wonderful rush of power and this joyful force of life Itself.

Take me, I want you.

I love this, I love it with a sense of touching the profound depth in all things – because I have loved you with all that I am, sweet beloved of mine. I love it all. I love this ocean of life. I found freedom, sweet freedom.

I love you, for always and forever –

Holy Gospel of Jesus Christ According to Saint Luke (10:21-24) "Jesus rejoiced in the Holy Spirit and said, 'I give you praise, Father, Lord of heaven and earth, for although you have hidden these things from the wise and the learned you have revealed them to the childlike. Yes, Father, such has been your gracious will.

Music, Metaphor and Magic

The beauty of this Self discovery is that we find ourself back in the world, renewed and full of youthful exuberance and joy. From *A Guide to Awareness and Tranquillity*, William Samuel explains this and more:

"The musician begins with the principle of music, not the discord. The mathematician begins with the principle of his science, not the error. WE BEGIN AS THE IMMACULATE, PRISTINE, PURE AND PERFECT IDENTITY WE ARE ALREADY, not the personal sense of things, not the world's ideas, opinions and judgement of things. We 'begin' with God, the

192

ALL that Isness is, and rejoice at the wonders this ever new view reveals. We LET that Mind be us which IS the awareness of the Truth we are.

"Awareness is the common denominator which includes ALL.

"Nor is Awareness separate from the images within it, any more than the television screen is separate from the cowboys and commercials there. Therefore, we can see that our identification as awareness ITSELF is not a withdrawal from the world, from people or from the adventure of living. It is a withdrawal from our own valued opinions, notions and prejudices of them.

"To the contrary, this work appears as revitalized interest in everything that appears as conscious identity (Awareness) – and that is everything! As we live childlike-awareness-being-effortlessly-aware, we find our daily experience expanding into undreamed of new action – plus the strength and means necessary for that action. Music comes from the principle of music. Music has an unseen fact behind it. That makes music a lot like God. God may just be the principle of music. That seems most likely.

"Music, like God, is a principle that can never be diminished. No matter how many songs are played the principle never runs out. God is the never ending Principle. Like music. I can make as much music as I like, write as many songs as I like, play as many tunes as I want and there is always more.

"If the sheet of music is torn up the source, the principle is still perfectly whole.

"The music exists because there is an unseen, untouchable, illimitable principle behind the music. Music is beyond the chords and beyond the notes and beyond the instruments used to play the tune. But the music I hear is the tangible evidence of something I cannot see and something that is an absolute fact."

Eight

4 A.M.

It is 4 A.M. and I woke up in total love. I feel the presence of a deep, warm light that is with me. I am immersed in the totality of love. I see the moon outside glowing bright.

This time of night touches me deeply with *something holy.*

Sweet mystery, that's what life is, a sweet mystery.

The light seems to be telling me I should write something.

Writing at this hour of the night could be dangerous. There is that uninhibited dreaminess that comes at these hours. I'll trust what this loving light unleashes.

I don't know much, but I do know I am totally in love with life. And so, I trust life to do me right. It always does.

This is also why I know I can't get hurt, or if I do, I don't care. I like to take my chances. It's a lot more fun that way. Wherever things go it is simply the joyful outcome of some road that just showed up. Roads show up. We don't have to go looking for them.

I have found my heart and my soul. That has been my savior. So I am letting life hold me and letting it take me.

Who can resist this holy delight of life's embrace?

It's been many years now that this light has been waking me up at these sweet hours of the night. I am led to interesting places, always transcendent and other worldly.

Oh, and here is something remarkable; this light continues to grow, expand, show me more, take me to the edges of time, take me where time ends and love lives eternal. It takes me to the heavenly realms of your warm, strong body in mine.

I find you here. Love does not end. Life gives in this unfolding intimate love for me. You came to me and the Truth is now established in my heart. Everything is wonderful. I am fearless. This that you brought me is powerful and exciting.

I am that little girl I used to be. She has returned to me. I love her passionate beauty that stirs me and lifts me high.

Well, now I am in pure bliss, as life is opening me to myself. I feel its presence here in this early morning holy radiance that I awaken to.

I am dazzled to just be here. You in me and I in you. Dear Life. Could Life be more sensuous, passionate, pleasurable than this? Could it be closer than this?

So trusting, life is easy. Nothing to fear. It's all good. And life just gives me what I need and I don't even need to know what I need.

I find myself. I find the mystic here. She is me.

There is a place, a secret place, where the sacred waters flow in sweet wanting of you. It all flows as you want me. I give myself to you.

Yes, I may have gone over the edge, but I really don't care. This freedom has taken my hand and love leads the way. How can I go wrong?

Giving to God what is God's, giving to my world what is only God's to give – my honest heart, my soul. I give my love to you. You can have it all – everything. It's all about giving.

Rather Amused

I was so surprised. This Child that returned was certainly not what I had been looking for nor expected in my search for Truth. And yet, when I found It, I knew this was It. There was no doubt about it. I had come home to myself. The one I thought I'd lost forever. She came back.

How did this happen? I have no idea.

I let it. I just opened my heart totally, then Life swept in and picked me up in laughter and joy and delight. I fell so tenderly in love. And then I became rather amused, funny and daring. That was really a surprise, a very wonderful surprise.

I have tapped into a holy wellspring. Lucky girl. Yes, one lucky girl. I am getting younger all the time. It's just wild. This living spark of fire just infuses me with enthusiasm and vitality. I think perhaps this is the Fountain of Youth that the explorers were looking for.

Too bad for ol' Ponce DeLeon, had he only known, he could have turned around and found it right there within himself. The Fountain of Youth is within us. Lord only knows.

Life, right up close, I am interfacing with life itself. This is where the creative, unleashed heart flows out from. This is where the living waters are, here within myself. Here I find all the unending colors. Here is the extraordinary beauty of my un-bridled spirit flowing from the soul of this unbound, innocent, purity that is the very life-force, vitality Itself.

Well, yes, I *have* fallen in love with Life and It *has* fallen for me. How could Life resist? I am adorable and soft and – well – funny too. Over the years we have become very close, Life and me. Life has taken me to so many strange and wonderful places. I feel It and It feels me.

Yes, Life has awakened me. This Holy Self of my heart feels it all. My senses are open and exposed to the ever-present beauty of this experience. I taste it. I touch it. I feel it. I invite it. I want it — and it comes into me and moves me deeply. I am enlivened by the flow of life as it touches every part of me. Seeing, being, knowing, doing, every action is love.

True security is not in the tangible things, not in the world of time and matter. True security comes from within our own heart and soul. True freedom is fearless and lives from the un-bound soul's love for living this sweet presence of Life. True freedom arrives individually for each of us as we find and live our soul's purpose here in the world. True freedom is this state of fearlessness, understanding what is before us. True freedom can't be found through indoctrination nor in the collective. True freedom is found in the heart, alone and individually.

Everything will be changed externally in this tangible world when each of us returns to the authentic inner freedom of the Child, recognizing the Unbound Light we are.

To find fearlessness in our own life, we live knowing where our true power comes from. Finding the one Light that is our very own all-inclusive totality and reality allows us to become faithful to our own authority, the Self we are. This is where the real revolution happens, inside each of us, in our soul, in our own self-discovery and recovery.

Rebels, heretics, iconoclasts, we should all become rebels who break from the arrogance and audacity of those who try to control others and control Life. Life is sweet. Life is holy. Life is Love. Control is not Love.

The Open Meadow

I have returned to the magical meadow. I have found this Self, the sense of Identity I am, and the world I live in, they are one and the same.

Now, as I find myself in my wholeness, I find myself in a slightly new, slightly mystical place right here in the very middle of the world I live in. I find the veil between this mysterious place, this secret garden, this other dimension, is lifted and I am in the Meadow playing, laughing, loving with you.

This magic is powerful. It fills me with something steady and bold and brave. I don't know where it is going, but I'll see what happens. I'll find out. I'll go with you over these grassy green hills. I'll enjoy this ride. I'll roll the dice and take my chances.

Life is magic. I am following all the strange things that go scampering past me. I am just here to see where it all leads me.

So far, this magical journey of my heart keeps bringing some most amazing wonderful surprises.

Here in the middle of the night, I feel you near me. I wonder if you would like to come sailing with me?

Let's sail over the sea of a starry night, sail across all time to the very far away where time ends. That's where we could go. Take my hand, let's fly. Let's go. Gliding along the Milky Way, through the glittering, sparkling diamonds that scatter their twinkling array across the heavenly dark velvet depths of Infinity. I catch that gleam in your desirous eyes, shining like the starlight. I see that sparkle of your inviting smile reflected in my eyes – it sinks down sweetly and takes me gently into my heart where Love lives forever.

I Love you always –

Silver Sparks

There I was riding my bike down the street. The day was kind of rainy, well, dark and misty, but no rain yet. I am just pleasantly riding along. The eucalyptus trees always give off this lovely distinctive fragrance, pungent, spicy, fresh, savory and satisfying when the air is wet.

I didn't realize I was in a daze, enthralled by this little bike ride. Every sensation in my body and mind and soul seemed to be awake. I was riding through heaven. I was taking it all in. All of it. The whole magical adventure just kept inundating and permeating every cell of my being. I was captivated by the beauty, the exquisite powerful sensuality.

Then, there it was, I wanted more. I wanted to be enveloped in this pleasure. It was like opium. Intoxicated by the sensuous delights, I was in love with everything.

I was so enamored with the beauty, the twinkle of the misty light flashing through the leaves, blinking on and off in golden and silver sparks of illumination.

Not realizing it, I had been captivated. Then I felt the wobble and wonk.

It only lasted a moment, but let me tell you, I became quickly aware that I was about to throw myself off course. Perhaps land in a ditch, lay the bike over, spill in the mud. It was subtle, the loss of balance, ever so slight, but enough to get my attention.

I love my ability to catch myself in slow motion. I love my equanimity. I love my skills in being able to make a quick change of direction, a little smooth maneuvering – that sweet bike and I, we were once again going fine.

This is the way about me, to be soft and supple, but very strong. Life on the road – or perhaps I should say *this road of life* – is more likely to evoke laughter and a gentle amusement in me than anything close to force or aggression.

Yes, I had lost my balance for a moment. Since I am sensitive to little changes, a new sound, a shift in the air, it does not take much to feel the nudge.

Those wobbles are so important along the way. I learn. And Life is all about learning. Learning how to ride this Road with the élan of being both strong and vulnerable, which sounds like a dichotomy — but, is not. I've learned to keep it lose and keep it tight both at the same time.

I can find the balance, to love the beauty and the powerful elixir of this unleashed spirit. But I must also realize that it can pull me into such a vortex of pleasure that I might get lost.

And yet, for me what's a little wobble — as I'd not have missed this sweet ride for anything.

The gods invited me to this party and I am sure not going to turn down an invitation from them.

However, I got the message. I won't lose my balance in all this beauty and pleasure and forget where I was going.

I will enjoy the marvel of this sensuous world of delights and keep my balance. I won't lose myself. It has taken me many years to find myself, and I am not giving her up.

I can enjoy the gorgeous scenery and ride with composure and grace, all at the same time.

At this point, I have found the way to ride and be enraptured by the passing scenery, while holding steady and true. I love my world mightily.

I can do it.

I used to be an expert skier. Well, I was good. I know how to keep my balance, and enjoy the beauty, both at the same time.

It takes being in control and powerful while also being open, giving, loose and easy. Life takes me on, I don't have to worry about it. It leads the way and I'll go with It.

How much I love my wondrous world. Feeling it all. I am having unprotected intercourse with Life. Feeling the whole sweet, passionate joy of Life. Fearlessly touching Life with my heart, my mind, my soul. All of me, take all of me, I'm in love. It is wonderful.

One has to feel the terrain while feeling one's own position all at once. I am good at this. I know how to love it all and take whatever comes.

I am, thank God, such a stalwart and strong hearted beauty. Oh yes, I know I am. Yes, I know how very beautiful and intelligent I am. And I am not reluctant to say so. I give God all the credit.

I am what Life made me as, and I am delighted by the Divine choice of qualities and attributes I was given. I maintain this deep equanimity. It is the inner place where I connect to God, the All in all.

I'll take what I got and do what I do. I trust my Self. That's where the real power is, right here trusting in this bright light of my Self. She is my guiding light. She knows where we are going, even when I don't.

And if I do take a spill or lose in my gamble, I am confident that it does not matter one bit. It makes no difference.

It is the ride, the joy of skiing on this holy mountain of life, the thrill of doing what I do.

Life and I, we are in love. Life looks at me and says, "You coming with me?" And I say, "Oh yes, you bet babe, I am. I'm right with you." We're going all the way.

Life and I are having a wild love affair.

It's absolutely divine.

I love you always, loyal and true – I thank you for all you have given me –

Ojai Serendipity

Many years before, when our children were very young, my husband and I would go to Ojai to listen to Krishnamurti speak in the Oak Grove.

One spring, when we were visiting Ojai, we went up to Krishnamurti's house on Thatcher to see if he was there. And to my surprise, he was. He came out of his house and came over to talk to me. He held my hand and said hello. I still remember how soft his hands were. I was so thrilled to see him and to have him holding my hand. We talked for a bit about everyday things. Then I just could not resist, guilelessly in tenderness for him, I said to him that I understood what he was teaching. He smiled and his eyes twinkled as he looked at me. I felt he actually appreciated my words. He held my hand tighter, saying very softly and clearly to me, "Yes, I see that you do."

There was a silence and then, still holding my hand, he asked me if I would like to join him and some friends for lunch. He was on his way to the main house where the party was awaiting his arrival.

Funny, who in the world would refuse that invitation? But I said no, that I had my husband and children there and they needed me, so I had to go. We said goodbye and I left.

I met Krishnamurti again a few years later, as my family and I often went to Ojai for little get-aways from the late spring snows in Aspen. He was on a walk with a group of people, and I was with my husband and kids. I stopped and said hello, we chatted a moment and he seemed delighted by my children and they with him — and there was not more than that. He had the heart of the Child, which was easy to see, a lighthearted innocence, a gentle and humorous charm.

Yes, life is magic. Things are synchronistic. We had always loved Ojai. Now our journey, twenty-five years later, led us back.

After a year in the San Diego mountains, Ojai would be our new place to settle. It would be our home. And it would be a mighty crescendo in this celestial song of destiny, serendipity and synchronicity.

Quantum Clockwork

In William Samuel's last book *The Child Within Us Lives!* he writes about time and that humans have a divine clock inside of them. A clock that is set to go off at a certain time.

From page 189 of his book:

"THE CLOCK IN QUANTUM MAN

"An inner Light tells me that people have clocks within them as certainly as the rest of the creatures in nature. We know something of this already. Puberty kicks in at a certain stage, then the mating and homing urges, et al, throughout our human span. But, listen, listen, something new and marvelous is presently happening to QUANTUM MANKIND. A new, worldwide 'urge' has begun. To this time in time, only a few have been made fully aware of this mystifying insight. A strange *new* disquiet and discontent. New urgings that have no rational explanation because they have never been felt by mankind at large, nor written of in words easily understood. We are seeing signs of this Divine Clock already in the bizarre behavior of this group and that. We've been blaming 'civilization' or television or something else for the strange twists and turns mankind has begun to perform internally and respond to externally. Recently we have taken to calling it anxiety, stress, informational overload and so forth. Something deeper is on the edge of exploding. The Divine Discontent that some of us have struggled with all our lives is soon to stir all humanity, bewildering all but those who know what it is and what is happening. Those who know are those who have had early access to these urgings and have responded in small ways.

"While all of us suspect there is more to life than the human scene, a universal recognition is sure to come that INDEED there IS Something Else — another dimension spread over the human experience. As we said, it is likely that science will confirm it first.

"THE CENTURY PLANT ILLUSTRATION

"Imagine a plant that has lived in the desert for nearly a century, then finally prepares to bloom, seed and die, its seed to begin another century of time. Imagine, also, that this plant has a winter's rest each year and new growth each spring — and has been doing this for ninety-nine years. Then, via a clock that has been inside that plant from the very seed it sprang from, it slowly — or suddenly — begins the epic event. It starts to grow a stem and a bud thereon.

"Can you imagine how the fragmented plant must be self-shaken by all this strange, new happening, so unaccustomed it is to blooming? The roots must wonder where they are supposed to send their nutrition NOW. The limbs wonder where the new growth is going — and why. The roots and leaves all send their substance into the new growth and finally to the flower itself. The leaves must complain that they are not receiving from the roots as before and the roots must wonder why the leaves are not giving to them as they have for ninety-nine years. 'Tradition is being destroyed! We must stop this foolishness and return to the old values!' This preparation of the bud is a shakingly new activity that embraces the plant now. The inner clock, dormant for ninety-nine years, has sprung into action and the century plant finally blooms, to seed and expire.

"The real bloom, for which the plant was originally intended, forms, blooms and carries the plant's essences and imprints into its seed-self. All the other spring 'bloomings,' the other cycles, the other events through the ninety-nine years have become as nothing compared to this final great blossoming which has been the purpose of the plant from the beginning – to prepare its seed for another field.

"What has happened for some of us individually is soon to happen for all mankind. There are two views we mortals contain – the individual view and the quantum overview; the man-with-a-name's view and the holistic view. From the standpoint of a View I have been blessed to live, I see clear indication that a new world clock has been turned on in the SPECIES – in the Quantum Man, exactly as God turned it on in what appears the individual 'me' forty years ago. Just as the century plant makes a final flowering at the end of its span, so the Tree of Life – appearing as humanity – is soon to begin a strange behavior from an unrelenting inner urge that will result, after much internal and external turmoil without precedent, in a New Bloom, a New Community. This divine stirring, different from all that has gone before in this pulse of events for eleven thousand years, will bring mankind to re-examine his values; rethink his ideas and belief; retest his religions and philosophies, his governments and systems, and find them woefully inadequate; thence to turn within himself into a subjective view of life, to discover the very Essence of Self-within – the Child of God.

"These events, already begun, will become quantum – every man alive feeling and responding, flailing positively or negative, responding in all ways, unable to find respite in the former things.

"THE INNER CLOCK AND THE WORLD TRAVAIL

"The world has begun the travail that ends in the birth of the
Child within – Messiah, Redeemer, Savior! – closer than
breathing, closer than fingers and toes, not far off but here all
the while. What is more, we will see THEN that this Event, the
'Birthing,' has every bit, each step of the way, been foreseen by
the lights and prophets, Eastern and Western, above and below,
first and last, male and female. More, all of this will be WON-
DERFUL – precisely what has been called for from the beginning – naught but GOOD going on – the REBIRTH of the
Original Image of Godhead.

"How do I know these things are true? I was shown all of this
wonder forty years ago at the pond and didn't believe a bit of it –
no way! – but, in the years since, having been faithful to the
Vision, having been tested by it and forced to live it, its veracity
PROVEN line upon line, precept upon precept, here a little,
there a little; and having found confirmation for every Glimpse
given, and having LIVED the Quantum of Mind as Awareness
confirmed – and tested by THAT – I have been told these many
years later to WRITE my findings to my inner Selfhood and
'prepare the way' for the Child's rebirthing and reappearance in
'the world.' I have done that as best I could.

"By the time this book is published, the 'quantum appearing' of the divine discontent will have kicked in for the world-at-
large. Not bad, but GOOD happening. The Child, the 'Children
of God' will survive."

I had always loved that section of William's book. It just
seemed to really touch some deep knowing inside of me. There
was no doubt and I could feel how this must be true. We are all
set to go off when our time is come.

Strange synchronicity – when we moved into our new home
here in Ojai, there was a century plant growing in the front yard

of the house next door. I could see it every day from our house. I don't think I had ever seen a century plant before. A few weeks after we moved into our new house, that century plant began to bloom. It felt auspicious. I kept thinking of William's story as I watched it bloom into a great big yellow-flowered stalk reaching straight up and out of the middle of the plant. I was delighted and awed to be the one to witness the wonder of such mystery.

Across the Sky

Laying in bed this morning, it was early, still dark out.

The window was open. I heard one bird chirping a little tune all by herself to no one. She was just pure happiness, pure joy, pure love, singing because she sings and she loves. Her beauty was evident. She loves the morning. She sings. The flowers and the trees and the sky and the air, they hear her singing. They hear her love song.

Something marvelous has happened. Beyond time, I become a mystic and a lover. I am powerful and rich with a joy and peace beyond reason and logic. I am alive and strong. I am unfolding, younger every day. I am feeling tender, vulnerable, easy, soft and yielding.

What is this place? My world is new. A new dimension has opened up to me. I am on the loose and I don't care. I am free. This revolutionary beauty. Who did this to me? Why did this happen? I don't know, but I will take it. I love this wild girl and the strange ride I am on. I will grab this lucky star of mine and ride it across the sky. I can't stop now. I can't turn around. I can't go back. I can only hold on — soaring into the infinite.

I can't do anything but to let it rocket me into oblivion. I hold onto this flash of comet that suddenly swept me up on a hot summer night when the sky was filled with a shattering, dazzling, shower of lights. It all came pouring down to earth that night. I caught that luminous tail as it flew by and I rode it disappearing into the deep, dark velvet cosmos.

All my Love –

And Because

Oh, this letter from William was grand too, so profound. His recognition of my life in the future was so clear. How did he see so much? I don't know, but reading it again, I soaked up the beautiful message.

"December 29, 1980
"I don't think this will reach you by the regular Christmas date, dear Sandy Jones......
.......But it will reach you by the REAL Christmas time. And, if I had been tending shop the way I should, you'd have been certain to hear from me months ago......

"because I write those I love
and because I write those who say 'Wow! Something happened!'
and because I write the Childlike
and because I write those who are experiencing
all I've experienced
and because I write to those who are brave and will to give up
everything to find themselves.

"Letters have been few and far between from me because I've been battling for a human life during the past year or so and my efforts have been to just hang on and hope for a few more times at the typewriter with enough inspiration to make a few more honest paragraphs about the long years of hanging on......

......and discovering......

......and finding out about the 'hanging on'......

"but there are those letters that seem to demand answers no matter what and yours most definitely fall into that category. So, I answer as best I can.

"Your words indicate you've made the 'breakthrough.' They say that you, like the rest of us – yet so very few of us – will be carried down this River of Light to be taken straight to the Ocean, the finding, the goal, the rest, the Shekinah. 'There really IS only One!' you wrote – and THAT is So! When your heart revealed THAT, you were not instructed by books or mortals – but by the Spirit within – the Life being You.

"The travel on the River of Life isn't easy – but you will MAKE it. More, you will chart <u>your</u> course and mark it on <u>your own charts</u> so that others can make the twists and turns beyond the shallows and sand bars and old shoals where the rocks are. Please, Sandy, keep a journal where your lightest, brightest – and darkest – moments are recorded. Such a journal will serve you well in the years ahead when it comes your time to help some group of wary travelers down the Way. Will you please do that? If you have ever been here for instruction you'd most surely have been encouraged to write – examine yourself via your own words and ideas. For you, there will never be words more important ANYWHERE than the words that come from yourself – written or spoken.

"Very much honest love to you, Bill"

I didn't know it, I didn't know then, but I had reached the Rubicon. All the prophetic words throughout William's letters were about to come to fruition and everything I had learned was about to be tried, tested and found faithful.

Nine

Black Leathers

He wore black leathers and knee-high boots as he straddled his beautiful new, red Ducati.

He adored me. Yes, I feel beautiful all the time because he loves me.

So many years married to him and I am still his girl. He is my angelic, magical man. There is something about him that is not of this world. Everyone knows it.

He has finesse. He has grace. He has style. He is charming and handsome and so very loving and kind. A rare gem, he is a genuine good and gracious man.

I think he came into my life as a gift from God, especially for me. I think I was granted a wish come true. A true love story. It was my destiny all along. I adore him. He is my real life Prince Charming. I am always in love with him.

He came into my life at the right time those many years ago. He gave me everything I needed and all that I wanted. There was never any doubt that all this was predestined by some divine story created just for me, just for us, just for all this unfolding beauty that spreads the Love everywhere. He was my soul's providence coming to me as a powerful Love manifesting in this magical world experience.

Faithfully he cared for his little family, for each of us, gently, tenderly, all those years. He was my heart, he was my soul, he was my life, he was my own cherished beloved part of me. I could not live without him, that I knew.

Kisses, all those sweet kisses. I love kissing him. I love him. I have loved him every minute of every day.

He was handsome, lean, strong and kind. His touch, his skin, his lips, his heart I treasured. He was always good to me. Always giving, giving to me. He adores our three children. And they adore him.

Yes, after all those years together he still attracted me, I wanted him close, I wanted him deep within me, within my soul, my heart and my body. I could not resist him. My arms, my lips were always wanting to touch him, be close to him, kiss him.

His family, us, we were his life as much as he was ours. It was clear that this was so. He was always with us one way or another. He was always near to us, always there, in some way. The sense of security he gave me was powerful in our relationship. I knew I was safe in his love. He was taking care of us, providing for us and protecting us.

I gave him my heart and he gave me his. I gave him my love and my faithful devotion as he gave me his. I gave him my protection, my strength and care as he gave me his. We were like those geese that mate for life.

Yes, we had it all. Yes, we did. We lived the perfect fairytale romance, the ideal love story, the joy of wedded bliss – we did indeed complete each other.

There he was, on his red racing Ducati, ready for an afternoon ride out along the winding mountain roads. He loved his motorcycles. He had a nice little collection. Among them, an older classic Ducati and a rare, vintage Moto Guzzi.

He looked so gorgeous in his black leathers. I went over, leaned in, put my arms around his neck and kissed him goodbye before he put his helmet on.

I watched him leave, waving goodbye. He had this charmingly attractive way of signaling me back as he would drive off. He would wave with a cool, easy flip of his right hand in the black glove and that elegant way his index finger would flash a friendly but sexy motion; cool, relaxed, confident and easy.

Thinking about him, he had a smile I could not resist. That little up-turn curl at the left side of his beautiful, sweet Libran bow lips.

I'd kissed him a million times and every time I got a rush, a flutter would run through me. I told him I loved him every day and every day I loved him more.

And he rode off. It was late in the afternoon.

Yes, I knew it was a dangerous sport. But he loved it. He had been a race car driver years ago. His love for speed, for racing, was who he was and much of what attracted me to him.

He loved to ride fast and lean the bike almost on its side. He was very good. He was in fine shape, agile and daring. He had a black belt in Tae Kwon Do. He was strong. I knew all that. I still worried. He enjoyed the feeling of being out on the roads, free and moving fast. He loved the speed and riding the twisting mountain roads. He loved the feeling of that motorcycle moving with grace and skill. I understood all that, and loved him for all that beauty he was.

Somewhere out there on that late afternoon ride, he must have reached the speed of Light and then — breaking the speed of Light — he rode right on through to the other side.

And I found out that Love never dies. I found out that the last enemy to be destroyed is death. And so it was.

Life and Death

There is no death, this I know for certain. This I found out by being face to face with death. Death is not what it appears to be, and neither is Life. They are both not what they seem.

The night he died, I died, everything died.

It all died. He was my life.

I was in shock, I couldn't maneuver this. I couldn't look at this. I could not accept this, I could not understand. And yet, there it was, the truth was that he was gone.

It was all real, and it was unreal. I could not change it. I could not bring him back. I could not do anything. I was face to face with death, but strangely enough I was face to face with Life at the same time. Face to face with Reality and Truth and unreality, what is not and never was – all at the same time. I saw it all, and saw it all from some strange world I'd never been to, a world where both sides became one.

The one person in my life to help me through this devastating loss, the one person who could comfort me, who could hold me, the one person I had always turned to for a soft place to cry, for strong arms to make things all right, the one person I turned to to feel safe, was the one person, my beautiful husband, who was no longer here to hold me and help me through my pain and sorrow and fear. I was alone. Completely, totally alone. I was on my own. Everything was over. I was totally alone.

As the days went by, things only got worse. The pain was felt in everything. Everywhere I looked there was an emptiness. I couldn't find him. I kept expecting the sound of the front gate to clang as if he was coming home. I kept looking for him when I walked to town, thinking I might see him there, meeting me on the street, finding me.

This was the end. This was unexpected and unacceptable. This was my point of true faith lived or not. This was where I had to make the final leap. This loss was my final undoing and my last battle.

I wept. I truly wept from the very core of Life itself, from the depth of my soul. The pain of loss was immense. I wept from a depth so profound it was as if love a thousand years old and all of eternity was inside of me. So many tears, such endless tears welled up and poured forth in the agony of this loss. The tears came like waves on the ocean. They would ebb and flow but they would not stop.

My beautiful heart was ripped open and yet every day I lived. Every day came and every day I had to face it all alone. I was still here.

The sense of loss was with me in everything. Everywhere I went reminded me how alone I was. I could hardly go out. I could hardly move. I had died but I was still here.

Every morning I was surprised to still be alive. I thought I would be like those loving couples where the widow dies only a few days after the mate dies.

But, no, every day I was still here. Nothing took me in the night. I would awake to face the days alone. I could only look directly at Life. I had nothing between me and Reality, me and Life and me and death.

The little things I'd taken for *just the way we were* became enormous holes in my world, no one next to me in bed at night, no one snuggling close, no one holding me in those early morning hours making love to me. No one there. The silence of the kitchen at sunrise without the hiss of the espresso machine as he made me a hot, double shot cappuccino. The amplitude of the emptiness permeated everything. I was adrift and floating and no one could rescue me, no one but me.

The silence, the loss, was so painful. No one there. No one to tell of this pain and no one to help me with this broken heart.

It was true, he had always stood in front of me. I had stood behind him, feeling safe from the world. I let him lead us. I trusted him so very much. He did have a certain magic about him and he always seemed to make the right choices. I was not an out-there, up-front person. I liked being hidden. I liked being the behind the scenes quiet one.

Now, I was facing myself and my world all alone. My buffer, my shield, was gone. I was pushed to the forefront, pushed into the world that I had been protected from.

And then, right there, in the middle of all this agony of loss, were our children. They had lost their father, the one who led the way, the man they cherished deeply and still needed. He was their sense of security and reliability in the world, just as he was mine. I had to be strong for them. Anything less would just add to their pain. I could not be him, though I wanted to. I could only stand brave in my own way, and do it for love, for them, for their precious hearts and souls that were completely devastated by this loss. I did my best and I lifted them up to the Light with me, as I lifted myself.

I was still here. I was still breathing and still alive. The days kept coming and I had to live them.

I don't know what I did those days and months. I just lived them. I just got up every day and got through the day. Somehow I lived.

However, in my heart I had a covenant that I knew I had to keep. There was Something extraordinary with me. There was a Light that held my hand. There was a Knowing Presence that would not leave me, a knowing that Life is Good and God is the very Light and Life of me.

There was this deep inner understanding that I could not drop down, that I had to keep my promise. I could not back out of the deal. I would follow through and remain loyal and true to this Light that was with me. I could not enter into darkness, for if I did, I would be swallowed up in that pit of hell and misery for an eternity. That feeling was so strong, and powerful. I had to stay far away from that abyss, far away from the things I knew were not true, were never true, were not real.

As painful as it was, I would not let the Light of Love and Truth go out. I had a deep sense that I must do this right. I had to Live this loss from the highest vision I was given to see. That vision was real, there is no death, I saw it so clearly when I saw him die. I knew he was not gone. I knew, I saw, I was shown, it was clear to me that he had not died, that his life was still Life and he was alright wherever he was. I so clearly saw that there is no death. I saw that death is impossible. Impossible. And though I was alone and he was not there, still I stood by my heart, the Truth that I had seen.

I was given a choice. This I could see. This was clear to me. I could drop down, I could wallow in self-pity if I wanted to. But I would not do it. I would not. I knew if I went down that road, I would never return. I would be selling out. I would be a liar and a cheat. I would not be honoring this loss for the Love it really was. I would have turned my back on my own self, my own heart.

I knew I had to do what was honest and right. I would lift my heart and soul and mind to the Light and I would do my best to use this loss for Good, to see the Good, to find the Good, to open my heart entirely to Life – to this Life that I knew now was truly Life Eternal.

Mixed in all these layers of loss and Love, I felt my beloved say to me that if I wanted to be near him, he was with the Light, and so I would have to stay with the Light if I wanted to stay with him. *When you think you have lost sight of me, remember I am in the Light, the Light that is Life.* He called to me. He coaxed my heart upward toward him. I felt him, I felt the Light, I felt where he was, and I knew I had to live my life uplifted close to where he was and not drop down, never drop down.

Something said to me, I better make this worth everything I have, because the loss was, for me, too much unless I lived it for Good, for Love, for the Truth that Life is Eternal.

After lifetimes of learning, it was now my time to step forth and do what I was here to do.

I knew in my heart my husband was fine. I knew there is no death. I knew that God is good. I knew that Love never dies. So for all of this love that was always with me, I had no excuse to feel sorry for myself, none. I could not and would not give into darkness, I would not do that.

I would not and could not close my heart down. Not now, not now that my heart was torn so wide open that the whole world was pouring in and through me. This was when I had to leap through that open door.

Something holy and miraculous was going on. The flow of Love and Life was moving through me, even in the raw unknown of this unfamiliar place. The pain was exquisite, holy, divine. I was being purified, washed with God's pure waters of Life, and I began to see it all. I knew what was moving me. I knew I was to become the strong, independent spirit, alone, solitary, single and whole. For this lifetime that I had been given, I must live from out of that beautiful vision of Life Eternal, and give that vision back to the ones I love, to my children, and to my world.

And so, through my tears and heart-break and fear, I stayed lifted up. I stayed with the Light and I stayed with my Love and with the Truth that had been revealed to me. There is no death. Death is not real. Life can never die. *We are not the body. We are the infinity of God's Ever Present Love.*

I stayed close to the place where my husband would come hold me and show me things. I stayed near to him by keeping my heart open and I let Life pour in and I let Life pour through me and I felt it all. I felt the glory of God in me. I felt the power and surge of angels. And the Light from heaven was holding me and taking me through the days.

I was living every day standing in the portal between this world and the "other." I was right there next to both sides of Life, and I could see death is impossible. I could see it plainly. I had the living proof for myself. This knowing has kept me whole, fearless and in love ever since.

Torn wide open, so wide the whole world flows through this vast and edgeless portal that I had become. And I know what Love is.

I recalled something William said, "Show me a revelation of Light and I'll show you a traumatic event from which that Light emerged."

And so it was.

And so I lived and trusted and the Light emerged. It did. Life came and took my hand, and held me. And I let It, and It took me, and we did it.

I Loved on. Love went on. Life didn't die.
Yes, I Loved on the same. And I kept on Loving.

Sailing

Tell me what is your latest revelation? Tell me what things of Life and Light and Truth have been revealed to you in these passing days that I have been out sailing the deep blue seas.

I was so far away, so far from land that I could not even communicate with anyone. I'd lost all contact with the old world I had left behind – and so you didn't hear from me for ages.

I sailed a long time. Yet out there on that wild and stormy sea, I did eventually come to new lands. I did find a new world. It is a strange and wonderful world, a world filled and brimming with treasures like an exotic market in some bustling, vibrant city. Colors are rich and bright, deep and pure. The Light shines here upon everything. The Light is in my eyes. My eyes sparkle and dance with Beauty.

Yes, I have been on a long journey, a very long journey, and I am returning home now.

I had a most remarkable time, in fact it was extraordinary, dangerous, treacherous, wild. It was a journey filled with pain, and light and beauty all at once.

Passion, the real true, heart opening passion, passion took me down, took me out, and then took me up and took me home.

It was mystical and magical, and yet, with all that it was, it was filled with a sorrow so deep, a weeping sorrow so immensely deep. And I was lost.

Although, glory be to God, that glimmering light house in the distance never left my sights. Even on the foggiest of dark nights, the light could be seen dimly in the mist. Pure comfort to know it was always there. Not that I could reach it, but that it was there, shining in the distance, comforting me across the sea.

I must tell you, this journey was the perfect agony of passion and aloneness that opened the way to another world.

I went to places that only a rare few get to go. Because the price demanded is not one that many are willing to pay.

Oh, but, I would not have ever paid such a price – never – no, not willingly. My payment had to be ripped away from my clutching, possessive, jealous, fearful grasp.

The payment was torn away from me, taken suddenly, stolen from me and I could do nothing about it.

As all hell broke loose, everything died. I died too.

Payment made. It wanted my life, it took my life.

So why not just see what this enormously costly ticket was for. I went, I just went. I had nothing to lose at that point. I climbed in my boat and I went sailing.

Then, it was not long out there on these unknown seas when I felt this wondrous thing begin to happen – love began to billow my sails. Love moved me along. Love held my boat from sinking. Love blew sweetly here upon this ocean and I could feel it gently pushing me along. I knew this silent zephyr of love would lead the way. No doubts. But, I had no idea to where it wanted to go.

I let go, I sailed on. I trusted the sky, the wind, the waters, the distant sounds.

No matter how rough the sea, love filled my sails. The misty salt air was all around, even in my heart. The salty waters of the vast, limitless ocean were the tears of an endless Love pouring from my Soul. I sailed upon an ocean of tears. Love never left my side, it caressed my being and it blew me away. It blew me into wondrous, foreign lands.

Love knows everything. Love came to me. Love did not and has not left me since.

It was a long journey, but now I am returning. The familiar land I had left behind is coming into view. The land I left is the same, but I am not.

I am happy to tell you I have brought you many wonderful gifts that I found while in those foreign lands. I am bringing them to give to you, my love.

Were you awaiting my return?

When the time is right, I will start unwrapping my souvenirs. You can look through them, and you can have whatever ones you might want. They are all for you.

Yes, yes! It is all true. Everything they say, it's true.

Life is Beautiful.

What would you like? Take, take it all. There is more where this comes from.

Since I have made the trip, I can now venture out into the deep any time I feel like it. I know what's there, I know the sea, I know the depths and endless infinity of it all. I found the new lands of ancient myths and fantastic discoveries.

I know this too, I know this most assuredly, God sails here in my boat with me, silver moon light covers us, I am not alone. It is me, my heart and you My Love. We three are one. We are the Holy Trinity sailing on this infinite sea of Love.

Sailing this ocean blue, vast without end, far, far away we go.

Now, listen, if you ever find yourself unloosed from the docks, drifting from shore, here is something to remember: Gently, lightly, softly, easy, feel it, feel it, move with it. Don't be afraid. If you think you are lost, keep your sight of the distant light that beams from those shores unknown.

Oh yes, heed the fog horn's longing call. Follow that haunting, beautiful sound, that deep mournful song that moves down inside your soul. In the blind dark of night when you cannot see anything in the mist and murk, listen for the powerful, profound cry, that distant, sorrowful call. Follow it. And sing, and sing — and keep singing.

Be brave my sailor friends. Be brave. The Wild Lands of Glory and Love and Freedom do exist. Eventually you will see the sun rise and the sea will turn into a smooth turquoise blue, a sparkling jewel upon which you glide and ride and rock gently with. There is a new world and it will be discovered.

I bring you treasures and tell you of love. I will paint wonder-filled paintings for you that whisper the totality of Light and shine like the beauty you are, my love, yes, the beauty you are.

I will write the Child's song and sing a verse or two. I will make you laugh and smile your sweet smile. We will kiss, and we will hold each other close.

I will slip a little love note into your heart, a simple note which will read, "It makes no difference, all is well." Sail away, sail away.

Loving You Forever –

Butterfly

None of these revelations took place suddenly or fully at once.

Oh, yes, the road took me up and down, up again, and around again. But with each new turn around the mountain of Life, the climb upward showed me something new, something that didn't negate the previous view, but included it within the newer, higher view.

All this took time. All this took a lifetime. All this took ages. It took being torn apart and raw. It took being honest. It took being brave. It took giving up and it took holding on. It took it all and it took it all at once and it took it all slowly.

This Joy I have found, it didn't happen quickly. No, no, it was a long road, but always a road that led to sweet places in time, moments of Peace and Love and Truth and Beauty. There was always some lesson, some learning on how to do better, how to live what I was seeing. I had to put it all to the test, doing it, living what I had seen from each new vista. Learning, learning, and testing, and proving. It took honesty with myself – all that I tell you I found.

But, I must say, when I discovered for certain, when I was shown the absolute fact that there is no death, I think that was truly the end of the search. That was True Liberation delivered to me. That was when the two became One. That was when the butterfly began to fly completely free from the bounds of earth.

A sweet seed so profound and so powerful, a seed was planted, settled softly into my heart many years ago and it grew a Tree here, a Tree that bloomed full of flowers. Flowers that eventually turned to fruit. It was the seed of the Tree of Life.

Here is what I love the best of all, it will happen for you in your own way, not like my way, but very specially in your own way, just for you, in ways only you will understand and know the reasons for.

I love you always –

Life Everlasting

From *The Child Within Us Lives!* William Samuel writes:

"Now in these late days when the final trump is sounded we will find and know the Messiah within the heart of ourselves. The Truth arrives, the second coming of Christ is the discovery that we are the Living Original Christ-Child of God, God's beloved and Only One. This is the New Covenant, the promise of Life everlasting.

"We can consider that certainly Isaiah foresaw the Child of God; (Isaiah 9:6) 'For to us a child is born, to us a son is given, and the government will be on his shoulders. And he will be called Wonderful Counselor, Mighty God, Everlasting Father, Prince of Peace.'

"The Christian ideology remains caught in buildings and numbers and refuses to listen to the Child Itself right in the heart of them.

"But, little do they realize they do have it right subjectively; The Child is the savior. A child shall lead a remnant of 'children' to the New Jerusalem, a new dimension.

"And be not conformed to this world: but be ye transformed by the renewing of your mind, that ye may prove what is that good, and acceptable, and perfect, will of God."

This is the Child within, the Self we are before the world was. This Original Nature is capable of showing us through this world. When you find this Prince of Peace, this guiding Light of your own heart and soul, you will be your own government and holy counselor. No more reliance on false idols. Your power will be found within. The fearless cannot be controlled or subjugated by fear.

Finding the real messiah within our very own self is to be born anew, pristine and pure in heart. This is, to me, the true meaning of resurrection and transfiguration.

For Something

When I read William's message the heart hears something wonderful that it has known intuitively from the first. The heart sings when I unleash and loose it from the old beliefs that tie and bind to sorrow and guilt. The heart soars because it knows its own beauty and freedom is already here.

"Gentle Sandy —
"Your letter of Jan. makes <u>much</u> sense to me. You are saying it <u>All</u> so well — yet, just as me, one often writes from the heart without really comprehending the beauty that has just been found and written.

"Your words have always told me that you have much <u>to Do</u> someday in the world. I don't know exactly what — but our 'suffering' and anguish — our Joy — are never for nothing! They are for <u>Something!</u> Watch and see.

"You tell me you know very well 'where 'I' (you) am' and you wrote it with grace and tenderness. I thank you so much.

"There is a 'Secret' few understand: What we tell ourselves, we tell our world.

"I've found it very true.

"Much honest love to you and yours, Bill"

Sweetness and Pleasure

And this sweetness and pleasure I speak of has nothing to do with those human pleasures that lack integrity, decency and honor.

No, this pleasure is decent, pure and guileless because this pristine heart of mine is made of gold. This is easy. This is real. This is genuine integrity, character, honesty and beauty. I know who I am. I stand true to myself alone.

To find and *live* the higher light of Intelligence is to know right from wrong and to fearlessly and boldly live fully from our strong heart. And I do. I am brave and I follow no one except my own heart's divine knowing. I am free. The child-heart of me has been restored. With this recovery comes lightened footsteps and a strong backbone, a heart filled with sunshine and laughter. I am the Child of God, the Son of God and I am my own authority. I have the Light here, as myself. I have found the true, fearless way. I have become the living joy of life itself. I have dominion.

Nothing to Lose

Come sail your ship into this safe harbor. I am here for you. I have nothing to lose. I have it all. I cannot lose anything. Life is all that is and It is divine. Life keeps me going. Life loves me and I love life.

There is the Child's world, and It needs no improving. It needs nothing fixed or learned, because it is already being quite perfect. Seems the more we try to improve the world, the more we spoil it. But, in truth we cannot spoil anything.

Not guilty, not ever. I will write of the real world I see, the one that is already perfect, right here behind time and space, people and things. And even though a room full of people are looking around at an imperfect world, I am still going to sing my song about this world of perfect beauty that they can't see. I should tell them It exists and that It is here. Even if they can't see it. They can't see without a change of heart.

I think, perhaps, maybe my words, my art, my love can bring about a sort of change of heart to those who seek peace and Truth. Maybe.

The Child's beauty, the joy I feel for life should certainly not be kept hidden. So, maybe others can hear and feel something ringing inside of them as I live and tell of this wonder and freedom we all really are.

Yes, there is something wonderful here, all around us and so few can see it. But there is this Child heart inside of us that can see it, and feel it and intuit it. I can't tell anyone about what I see, but I can try to find the words, and I can try to tell about it. I can get close. I know what comes from the heart can never be wrong. I do have the courage to say absolutely illogical things to logical people and that seems to touch that golden point, that listening heart in them, and I guess that is all I can do.

Serendipity: Luck that takes the form of finding
valuable or pleasant things that are not looked for.

Tears of the Heart

Yes, emotions, sweet feelings, the tenderness of the Child that knows how very beautiful these caring feelings are. The Child is not afraid of the feelings. The Child lets her heart and emotions flow freely. When life is lived, it is felt in the core, where we know who we are. Tears of joy, tears of love, tears of sorrow, it's all divine. In this *knowing* we are touched by the power and depth of living beauty. We find the center and the balance, but we don't eliminate our feelings, our emotions. In many ways we become even more tender, soft, and tearfully in love with everything.

Yes, sweet life, touch me, touch my soul, let me feel it all. I won't hide from life. I love my feelings, my tenderness, my tears, my joy, laughter, my exquisite loving sorrow.

I am alive and I feel this Life as the lover that comes into me, that touches me inside and out. I have no boundaries, I have no edges. I breathe the life and presence of God's holy being. Life is all that is. I have let go. I surrender to this Love. Knowing this

227

Lover that moves all things, I am swept up in the beauty of listening to this song of the Universe, the sweet sound of this heart of mine as the Universe entire.

This life is the life that God is. Freedom reigns here where the child-heart is. This heart is pristine. It is the original purity that was never dragged down, never hurt, and was never changed by anything harmful or dark. It remains untouched. It can be claimed, and when it is, it restores us to laughter and goodness and abiding peace.

Always and Forever, My Love —

Simplicity

Once upon a time God said to the angels, "Well, we all know that Truth is such a simple thing. We don't want it profaned. Where shall we hide it so it won't be found?"

One of the angels suggested hiding it in the ocean, because the ocean is big and deep, and it would be very hard to find.

God said, "No, sooner or later it will be found there."

Another angel said, "Let's hide it in the clouds somewhere, or on the Moon."

And God said, "No, because one of these days it will be found there too."

So He said, "The best place to hide Simplicity is to bury it deep within the intellect of mankind, because the intellect will never allow it to be found."

And so it is. The Truth and its Simplicity cannot be found by the intellect.

Sweet Simplicity. Only the innocent and childlike understand. Only the Heart can find It.

Your Heart knows —

Ten

Rockets

This Light of Life has given me a gentle and wise heart to see with.

This living soul of mine is not limited to time and space. In this world I soar free through this electric-blue of transcendent heavenly glory.

Life, this linear, material life, north and south, a two-way street, inside and outside, up and down — there are always two ways about it.

And then there is that holy third way. It goes unnoticed by most. The gold happens when the two are mixed just right. The third way appears.

When spirit and matter come into one, we find ourself living free. We are transformed. We become the three that are one. This, the Holy Trinity.

All this is right here. This life, with hot coffee on a cool and gentle evening.

Life includes a powerful depth of love so profound that it touches everything I do and see and be.

Well, here I am watching it all unfold.

I am so impressed by the magic of my life. Transformation and beauty comes to me.

It's an interwoven ride, up is down sometimes. As I rise above the world, my ascending brings me back into the world. I don't mind the twists and jolts that throw me around. I am so delighted by this wonder of being alive and unbound here in this world once again.

I am swept up in the crashing spins, the unexpected joy and laughing like a little girl again, ready for whatever next amazing sight or sound appears.

The key to it all was that I was given a heart that, years ago, was broken wide open, so open that the whole world can walk through now. I don't mind one bit. What I am inside is what I be. And what I be is what I see. I see Love and Beauty wherever I am.

The quantum reflection goes both ways.

That's how Beauty meets Beauty on the way to nowhere. I was blown wide open and in rushed all this sweet, unsolicited magic.

It was inevitable, but I didn't know that at the time.

That is how I met him.

That's how it happened, he was a rocket scientist, just knocking on my door late one night for reasons unknown.

I opened the door.

He asked me to come outside and watch him light the night sky.

I did –

– and he did.

He lit them all and I watched those flashing hot trajectories blow, scattering joy everywhere. So powerful the explosions, they went right through me and over the moon.

There was such glory and blasting heat and radiant colors hanging in the night air. I could do nothing but succumb to this beauty and wonder he offered me.

I was captivated by the bombs and the thundering symphony of sounds pounding the dark sky and pulsing through my body, my heart, my soul. The drums of explosions played all through the night.

I was so moved, I was swallowed up, engulfed in the show.

He enchanted me. I stood by him, so close and warm he was. We both laughed with joy at the sight of those rockets bursting in air.

Well, the scientist and his fireworks came and went as the stars began to fade and daylight glowed on the horizon. He was gone.

But the explosions still resound within me. The powerful intensity of the crescendos reached by that glorious symphony, even now, reverberate through me.

Yes, I was awakened in the middle of the night and now I cannot go back to sleep.

Those brilliant projectiles left a lovely golden residue drifting and sparkling in the air, landing like a halo in my hair. That halo still glitters and shines wherever I go.

The Light of those rockets so dazzled my eyes, I still see stars and glowing, flashing, twinkling magic wherever I look.

A sweet note in the melody of Life is to live in open expectation of Love's unending good showing up.

You won't know what it will be, and that is the wild joy of it all. That's the surprise party of it.

Like a child in happy anticipation of a birthday celebration, the good surprises will show up just the way they are meant to. And they will be made to order, especially for you.

As long as the stars are above you – I love you always –

Forever My Love

Curtains pushed aside, awakened by the storm, now the morning sun brings the light. I reside in this abiding peace. Pale pinks and greens shine their light among the twinkling blues and rich deep purple velvet of God's love.

I awaken to my Beloved.

I see now the butterfly cannot remember its time writhing in the cocoon.

God is good and love is the most powerful healing of the wounds. Such power that I can barely remember now the agony of the loss. I am free. I am alone and I am free and I am the joyful, triumphant Child.

Listening and knowing that today love holds my hand, love leads the way.

The perfume is everywhere, inside out and from outside in. I put flowers in vases, set them on the tables, and breath in this freshness of the morning, the new day.

Sweet With Easy

I go outside this morning. The rains drenched the dry, parched earth.

All night long the torrential rain poured its love upon the awaiting land. The water opens the earth's heart to bring forth new life.

It is the passion of earth and sky coming together. Now all is soft, wet, moist, green lush, soaked in the rich, sweet fragrance of unfolding beauty.

It is the power of this unrestrained force that performs such magic.

Do you remember when you were a little boy and I a little girl? I do. We had fun. Wild, unafraid, carefree, daring. That's the girl that has been released in me. She is the Light of my Life. And she stands quite solitary and alone. She returns as my sweet, easy, unbridled, lawless joy.

The jasmine over the doorway is bursting with white-pink blushed flowers. How quickly it all blooms.

Saturated now, your sacrifice has been noted. I see your holy light. I am most truly grateful that you came – and went. I cannot think of a more perfect love.

The fragrance of the flowering jasmine fills the morning air. The orange trees have come into bloom too. I am living in heaven. Scents of orange blossoms and jasmine sweetly drift through the air, and catch a golden gleam in the early morning light.

Love Forever –

Love's Mystery

Morning light sparkling through the trees outside my bed-room windows. Sweet fragrance of orange blossoms dance through the cool soft air. The glittering golden sunlight twinkles and flickers a love song to the leaves.

The kiss of beauty awakens me.

What Love this Life has been to me.

I am fully aware of this bounty and abundance that has been poured upon me and now it runs over the edges where I taste the honeyed nectars of Life.

Nothing but joy and love in all the ways it unfolds.

How delectable to be the prize of this sweet conquest.

How surrendered, open and giving I am to my victor.

I am the loyal friend, the faithful lover, the deepest Heart of a Holy Mystery.

I feel the exploding force of alchemy and synergy of Love and the power of Light as it penetrates the infinite beauty of the timeless depth of my soul.

Yes, always –

Change

This is what I love – I love standing on the shore of the big Pacific Ocean and letting the water rush in and swirl around my feet. I love that I am strong and steady and at ease with this mighty ocean.

I understand my mighty ocean and its tides. I feel it, I flow with it, I love it for its wild, powerful energy, and it loves me.

Like this sweet Life, nothing is always easy, but for me, the pure bliss of being here is perfect.

There is a Changeless Beauty here, steady, silent and true. Standing in this salty, rolling water, barefoot with toes nuzzled deep into the wet sand, the ocean pushes and pulls on me. It comes and goes. In and out, swaying me, moving me. I hold, I yield, I give, I receive.

Some days the waves break wild, crashing in full force as the water rushes in at me. Other days the sea is calm, serene, with small green waves playfully lapping the sandy shore.

I am ready for whatever the sea may bring to me. I will stand easy, giving and taking, letting it move me, watching its powerful beauty rush to shore and then take itself back leaving the land altered, ever changing and ever beautiful, by the force of each oncoming wave.

I love you always –

Know Thyself

Something very wonderful has happened. I am free. The end turns out to be the beginning.

The light is flickering, dancing through the leaves on the tree as I write. I am in love with Life. I love my world. This day is sweet and green, fresh and new. It is March and the spring time is blooming, birds singing and I am in love.

It is many years since these events I write of. Life continues to bring me more joy and increasing wonders every day.

It has been many years since I began that climb toward the top of this Mountain of Life. I did get there. I found the summit. From there I saw all life within me. I realize, though the journey is line upon line, precept upon precept, here a little there a little, in fact I was always here, always atop the world, always this bright, innocent, pristine, bubbly little girl.

Now, living it all on my own terms, listening to myself, I can do whatever I need to do right where I am, just as I am.

The world is not to be renounced. It is to be understood. The self is not to be renounced. It is to be understood.

In this place, right here where I walk, God is.

There is an old statement we have all heard: Know Thyself. That's because the only way to all that you long for is by way of this self that is made in the image of God. The only way to know is through yourself. The Unknowable God will be known through knowing the Self is made in Its image. Know Thyself, that is where the treasure is hidden. Closer than fingers and toes, it is your Self. *You* are the treasure.

The pathway to God, to understanding, is through the self where we come closest to God the Ineffable unknowable one. "I am the way, the truth and the life. No one comes to the Father except through me," doesn't mean through another someone else called Jesus, but through *me*. Through myself. How else can we say it? It is only through *me* that I can come to find, know, experience, feel the Living Light of God. That is quite correctly the only way to say it. Each one must acknowledge and claim this Light, the Child, for him/herself.

And the words "I and my Father are one, but my Father is greater than I." That too is a statement that applies not just to the man named Jesus, but *every man, woman and child,* every one of us. Just as Jesus was, I too am one with Life, one with God, and yet in this holy oneness, God is the Greater. The Child is the personal Christ within us. The Child is the comforter that comes when we love God with all our heart, as the Light, the Life, the Truth and the Way. This holy comforter abides with us forever in the spirit of All That Is, of Life Itself.

The journey is within. The world is within us, because there is only one Awareness being all that I am. The depth and infinity of the Self is the infinity of the Universe.

Our purpose for being here is about finding our Self and then being that Love in the world. Just being and living this Love. Love and Happiness is our reason for being. You will find this Love includes your broken heart, yourself just as you are. In this Love you will find the peace you long for. The real joy comes not from being self-less but being Love that loves this self as Life's Self Knowing Light. Life, you and me, we are the Living Love. We are the divine awareness of this all-inclusive Light of Life we are. We cannot be any other than This.

As this One Light of God is being all that I am, my whole world is here within me. God is Love and God is All that is. And when I find this Truth I find I am not alone at all, I am filled with every iota of everyone, and you and Life and the Infinite itself. Nothing is outside of Me. I don't leave life, I become all life. In this singleness and solitary sense of myself, I have more than I could ever have dreamed. I am filled with this unending bounty of friendships, of others who love me, others who bring such kindness. It is my pleasure to give all I can give. Generosity, happiness, laughter and love, the very nature of life itself, it is all here, seen and unseen. It is Life that moves all things.

I am here for all those in my life. My Source is endless and Infinite. And I am free because I am not afraid. Somehow the Light of this whole world is shining through me. It's all my Sweet Mystery, always present and always here.

The Child is holy. The Child is something like a portal, an open door between infinity and time. I stand here between the seen and the unseen and I see them both as one Life. When you make the two as one, that's when it happens. That's when the Joy comes fully alive again.

I know that the way for each of us is individual and unbound, that the path up the Mountain of Life to freedom and love and peace can only be traveled by each of us alone. The vision from the high place is for the alone. The willing go forward alone.

I am strong. I am full. I am rich. I can nurture and love and give my strength and comfort when it is right to do so. I can keep myself contained when it is not mine to give. I am discerning and discriminating in my own ways. I stand true to myself. The joy and blessing is in me. Just as It is in you. It is in everyone. We do this all by ourselves and this inner interface with ourself makes it our very own. Authentic knowing is here in our own soul. This bright, whole and happy Child is personal and it is Real. Being Real, the Child is untouched by time and matter. Now, as our unbound eternal light, our heart open and free, we understand and love our world with all our heart.

What I have written, why I have written, how I have written is to convey a direct realization of your true and natural identity, your eternal childlikeness. So that these words may gently enter the heart and you might recognize this Child Light of yourself. Yes, the Child lives. It may be hidden from you, you may feel it has vanished and that it is nowhere to be found. But the Child is still here. The Child is real, ready and waiting to return to your experience.

How can I prove that to you? I have proven it for myself – and I believe you can too.

With this tender light of truth, I have become empowered, I have dominion. My soul, my life is ageless. I am free. And I allow myself the permission to do it my way. I refuse to bow to the gatekeepers no matter how high on some bogus line of hierarchy they might deem themselves to be. I am fearless.

"When His disciples said, 'When will you be shown forth to us and when shall we behold you?' Jesus said, 'When you strip naked without being ashamed, and take your garments and put them under your feet like little children and tread upon them, then you will see the child of the Living One. And you will not be afraid.' " (*The Gospel of Thomas,* Saying 37)

This transcendent beauty and freedom I have found does not end. I continue to grow and learn. This pristine, unashamed Child I am is now in direct interface with the very living of this Light of Divine Intelligence. This faith is not faith in the world, not faith in humanity, not faith in things that come and go, but Living from the *Living Faith* that is this Presence of Life, God Itself. This is with me always. It is me. It is mine. This is the Immutable Heart and Soul of you too.

My love for you is deeper than the deep blue sea. My friends, we have much work to do and love to share.

I love you forever and always –

"The cosmic clock has clicked on and Everyman has begun to stir. The Synthesis is coming. A grand global harmony is just around the corner – the one the prophets spoke of wherein there is no more sighing, no more tears and no more fear nor need of temples and teachers.

"As it might be said in the East, the night of Brahman falls as soon as the harvest of the Seed is accomplished. The Morning of the New Day comes quickly." –William Samuel